Working with the Bilingual Community

NATIONAL CLEARINGHOUSE FOR BILINGUAL EDUCATION

This document is published by InterAmerica Research Associates, Inc., pursuant to contract NIE 400-77-0101 to operate the National Clearinghouse for Bilingual Education. The National Clearinghouse for Bilingual Education is jointly funded by the National Institute of Education and the Office of Bilingual Education and Minority Languages Affairs, U.S. Department of Education. Contractors undertaking such projects under government sponsorship are encouraged to express their judgment freely in professional and technical matters; the views expressed in this publication do not necessarily reflect the views of the sponsoring agencies.

InterAmerica Research Associates, Inc. d/b/a
National Clearinghouse for Bilingual Education
1300 Wilson Boulevard, Suite B2-11
Rosslyn, Virginia 22209
(703) 522-0710/(800) 336-4560

Library of Congress Catalog Card Number: 79-84372
ISBN: 0-89763-013-0
First printing 1979
Printed in USA

10   9   8   7   6   5   4   3

Contents

Foreword

Working with the Bilingual Community is a collection of five papers dealing with parental/community involvement in bilingual education. María Estela Brisk discusses the subject in light of legislative and judicial issues. María B. Cerda and Jean J. Schensul describe in detail a Chicago program designed to train parental leaders in the Hispanic community. Kennith York discusses the Mississippi Choctaw Bilingual Education Program and how parents and community members have contributed to its initiation, growth, and success. Norberto Cruz summarizes his recent research identifying roles and functions of parent advisory councils serving Title VII Spanish-English programs. In the final paper Alberto Ochoa examines the need for parental participation, presents three approaches for involving the community, and suggests activities for generating parental interest and support.

One of the functions of the National Clearinghouse for Bilingual Education is to publish documents addressing the specific information needs of the bilingual education field. We are pleased to add this collection of papers to our growing list of publications. Subsequent Clearinghouse products will similarly seek to contribute information and knowledge which can assist in the education of minority culture and language groups in the United States.

National Clearinghouse
for Bilingual Education

The Role of the Bilingual Community in Mandated Bilingual Education

María Estela Brisk

During the last two decades, bilingual education programs in the United States have evolved from a few locally initiated programs to programs supported by federal assistance under Title VII of the Elementary and Secondary Education Act and, more recently, to programs mandated by state legislation or court litigation.

Common to the first type of programs has been the involvement of ethnic and linguistic minorities in their initiation and planning. Discussions or negotiations between the educational establishment of a particular city (school administrators, school boards, and teachers) and language minorities, before a program has been created, have often led to an effective coalition that implements and monitors such programs.[1] Rallying around shared interests, such coalitions have recognized the varied benefits offered by bilingual education: broadened community participation in setting educational goals, realistic acceptance of pluralistic social and cultural objectives, recruitment of minorities into the teaching profession, and—most significant—improved academic performance of students at all levels.

It is generally accepted that well-planned bilingual education programs offer these and many other advantages that can be perceived by a wide audience. But it is not always recognized that the process of community involvement has made the difference between successful and merely ritualistic responses to the needs for such programs. In the case of mandated bilingual education, the participation of the community is varied, due to organizational and time constraints.

While most supporters of bilingual education have welcomed the gathering legislative and judicial support for bilingual education—as evidenced by new state laws, the repercussions of the Supreme Court decision in *Lau* vs. *Nichols* and the Office of Civil Rights guidelines that followed, and the connection between desegregation disputes and educational reform in many cities—there is a tendency to overlook one of the costs of such mandated efforts to pluralize education: a possible lack of community involvement.

This paper is reprinted from the CAL-ERIC/CLL Series on Language and Linguistics, Number 49 (1977), issued by the ERIC Clearinghouse on Languages and Linguistics, Center for Applied Linguistics, 1611 North Kent Street, Arlington, Virginia 22209. This paper is also available from ERIC, ED No. 138 086.

This process of involvement takes time, so it is important that it be initiated long before the actual mandate takes place. Otherwise, the rush to meet compliance guidelines can have negative effects on the quality and staying power of such reforms. In many cases, not enough time is allowed for an ethnic or language community to determine its own interests, and a hastily organized group may be produced which poorly represents community interests or does not reflect sound educational practices. Lack of a prior working relationship between the community and educators can be a source of friction, and efforts to get the two factions to agree to a common plan may fail for lack of empathy and common perceptions. Finally, there is a danger that the rush to comply will put a premium on general guidelines that do not take into consideration the unique social and educational patterns of each community.

It would be wrong to argue against efforts to mandate bilingual education. On the contrary, communities should take advantage of mandates in order to attain their educational goals, but they should be organized and cognizant of the issues, so that the resulting bilingual programs closely reflect what they believe is best for their children. Legislation related to bilingual education is only remedial in nature: it helps non-English-speaking children learn enough English to keep up with their monolingual English-speaking peers in the educational system. Community involvement and pressure can assist in the implementation of comprehensive programs that go beyond these minimal requirements to comply with the law.

Bilingual education already has considerable momentum. At least twenty-two states have enacted pertinent legislation.[2] As a result of the Lau decision, all school districts in the United States are required to submit periodic reports to the Office of Civil Rights that specify the types of programs they offer to children of linguistic minorities. A number of school districts have been found not to comply fully with general guidelines and have been forced to develop plans to service these children adequately. In Hartford, the bilingual community took advantage of the situation and developed a comprehensive plan for bilingual education with cooperation of the school board and the office of the superintendent. There have been other instances where parents of bilingual children have filed suit against their own school districts on the grounds that for lack of a coherent program, their children were receiving an inadequate education.

In order that their children's educational interests be considered in the midst of integration, bilingual communities have also entered as secondary parties in desegregation suits brought before federal courts by both the Department of Justice and private citizens. This intervention has been a crucial factor in avoiding the collapse of existing bilingual programs. Assigning youngsters to schools on the basis of ratios of black vs. white has been justified as a means of improving education. The needs of linguistic minorities, however, are ruled by linguistic and cultural characteristics and not by race. In order to have viable bilingual programs, an adequate number of children of the same ethnic group must by kept together, but this causes problems with desegregation.[3] In most cases, courts have ruled in favor of the bilingual population, but sometimes the wishes of the bilingual community have not been followed. In the case of Boston, for instance, although clustering of bilingual children was allowed, the courts did not permit the continuation of a special program for secondary school Hispanic children who were working well below grade level, because it was housed apart in a school with no children of other ethnic or racial groups.

State legislation, private suits, and desegregation proceedings have combined in some cities (New York, Boston, and Hartford, for example) to produce added pressure for bilingual programs. The rise of public-interest law firms throughout the United States will undoubtedly continue to spur such litigation in the future.[4]

It is the purpose of the present report to alert community organizers, school officials, and scholars to their mutual interest in securing community involvement in the planning and execution of bilingual programs. Strategies will be proposed for bilingual communities to follow when confronted with mandated bilingual education. The ideas expressed in this paper are the result of the author's work in the United States with several bilingual communities facing such a situation. The proposed process is not a theoretical model based on studies in community organization but, rather, a summary of successful strategies. The report will focus on the structure of the community and other interested parties, on the type of community organization required for effective action, and on the role of the community in setting goals for implementing and monitoring bilingual programs.

Participants in the Policy-Making Process

The Bilingual Community

The word "community" has many connotations. "Sociologists have grappled with the concept of community since Comte and before him, philosophers since Plato."[5] Panzetta describes three possible types of community: horizontal (geographic) community, whose members have a relationship of mutual dependency; a vertical (institutional) community, whose members have a formal relationship; and a third type, formed by a group of people who come together in common pursuit over a period of time. In the context of bilingual education in its broadest sense, the word "community" refers to the last-named type— a group of people interested in the development and improvement of the education of bilingual children. In its narrowest sense, it can refer to the parents of bilingual children attending a particular school. It is not the author's purpose in the present report to define the bilingual community, but rather to suggest how it can be most effective. Considering what Guskin and Ross have to say with respect to urban problems, the bilingual community that can exercise pressure and provide meaningful cooperation for improving education opportunities must be composed of a broad spectrum of people.

> The last few years of urban crises have generated a new concern about the citizen's role in the planning process. Given the complexity of the issues and the growing sophistication of techniques in urban and social planning, many writers have argued that community groups, especially in low income neighborhoods, need the expertise of professionals to defend their interests in the policy process.[6]

Family, neighbors, informal groups, professionals, and formal organizations all have an important and different role to play. Hence, for purposes of this report the word "community" refers to a coalition of all of the above components. The specific composition of a bilingual community will vary, depending upon the social and linguistic composition of the school district in question.

Two major problems arise in the proposed organization of the community. The first is the establishment of communication among the members of a community that is not necessarily geographically defined. The second is the establishment of good working relationships among the various types of groups involved. Ideally, all of the members of the community should be informed of the various issues in question and their opinions solicited. The size of the geographical area and the distribution of its members will determine the feasibility of this task. In the case of Boston, when faced with desegregation, the Hispanic community formed a committee with one representative from each of the city's seven districts that had concentrations of Hispanic populations. Throughout the process, every issue was discussed first in the central committee and then in district meetings, with the representative serving as a link between the two. This system allowed communication with the community without forcing people to travel long distances. Another advantage was that a committee of limited and fixed membership could work more efficiently than one that tried to cover the entire population, but whose meetings were seldom attended each time by the same people.

A committee that is going to organize the community for the defense of bilingual education should include "grass roots" members, professionals (including lawyers, school staff, researchers), and organizational representatives. The problem is to get these groups to work together. Lay persons often distrust professionals, while the latter often try to impose their opinions upon their "clients" without listening to what they have to say. Much effort is often wasted in struggling over power. The best strategy seems to be for the professionals to assume an advisory rather than a leadership role. Established organizations can help to disseminate information, offer meeting places, and secure funds. To avoid unnecessary conflict, the role of each component should be clearly defined during the initial meetings and the tasks divided according to who is best qualified to perform them. (The matter of allocating tasks will be discussed in detail in a later section of this paper.)

Educational Authorities and School Personnel

For many minority language communities, successful collaboration in policy making requires an understanding of the composition, leadership, interests, and constraints of the other groups involved. Situations differ from school district to school district, but the participants usually include a school board, a superintendent, monolingual administrators and teachers (often represented by one or more unions), and bilingual school personnel (who are also members of the bilingual community). The school board members and school superintendent are likely to be concerned with overall education objectives—which include serving bilingual children, but not necessarily through bilingual education—and are sensitive to their own budgetary constraints in planning new programs. Principals, teachers, and other personnel often perceive mandated bilingual education as a threat to their job security and to their own concept of education, especially if their mission includes "assimilation" of minority students.

The members of the bilingual community must be aware of the particular concerns of these sectors and must exercise great tact and skill in presenting the case for bilingual education. It should be kept in mind from the very beginning that implementation of any plan, even when mandated and upheld by the courts, will depend upon the good will and support of each sector involved. It is easier to ensure the support and understanding of school authorities for the cause of bilingual education when members of the bilingual community are part of the school structure or have working relationships with it.

Bilingual school personnel are likely to exhibit, as far as bilingual education is concerned, attitudes ranging from reticence to assertiveness. Most school systems that have attempted to meet the needs of minority language groups have established a special office which must respond to pressures from both the educational establishment on the one hand and vocal members of the bilingual community on the other. Some bilingual school personnel feel caught in the middle and resent undue pressures from parents of bilingual children and other advocates of bilingual education. Consequently, it is important that these persons be made a part of the community organization so that they may better understand the position of the parents as well as provide the community with their support and advice.

Community members may also exert influence through election or appointment to the formal educational structure, e.g., school boards, school administration, and advisory committees and task forces with policy-making power. In this way the interest of the bilingual child will be assured in decisions carried out by educational policy-making bodies.

Planning the Bilingual Program

Survey of School Children (Needs Assessment)

An assessment of needs is the first step in the planning of a bilingual program. Community organizations are in a unique position to survey and evaluate the broader language and educational needs of their own school-age children. Such a survey, including information on age, grade, school attendance, promotion history, and language skills (in English as well as other languages) may best be initiated at the local level. A bilingual community can often make use of the tools and expertise of its local organizations or scholars who, in turn, can train parents and other nonprofessionals, who usually have more accessibility to the community at large, to gather the information. Even if this type of survey cannot cover an entire city or employ sophisticated and scientific measures, it can provide far more meaningful and current data than that employed by school systems. This is especially true when, for convenience, school systems classify children into language groups simply according to surnames—an exceedingly rough and usually inaccurate measure of linguistic and education needs—or when monolingual teachers try to estimate students' verbal aptitude.

The primary purpose of a community survey is to produce information from which the community can determine its needs on the basis of actual rather than hypothetical data. In the case of Boston, the school committee and the school department's estimated number of children in need of bilingual education was markedly lower than the figure provided by an informal survey carried out by the "Comité de Padres." Fortunately, desegregation plan calculations on space and personnel needed for bilingual programs were based on the latter, which proved to be more accurate.

When the community is engaged in conducting such surveys, an additional benefit occurs. The broadened support from the community in the area surveyed may produce a new level of community consciousness and considerable volunteer help for later stages. Thus, the survey can become the first step toward community organization and participation.

On the basis of the information collected, the community can begin to discuss alternative approaches to planning bilingual programs and focus on realizable goals. In order to develop a plan, it is necessary to know the proportion of children at each age/grade level by neighborhood and with respect to the total school district. This will help establish the numbers of classes and teachers needed at each level and will help determine priorities. The linguistic ability of the children, i.e., language (English and other) and skill (speaking, understanding, reading, and writing), will suggest the type of language component needed. Data on the numbers of children not attending school and the reasons for their lack of attendance may suggest a need for special programs. For instance, the lack of bilingual kindergartens may keep children at home, or literacy problems may often account for dropouts.

In many cities, such surveys have uncovered information that has surprised school authorities. Distinctions may be found among students thought to be part of a homogeneous language group; for example, Asian American children may have been classified as "Chinese" despite the fact that the group may comprise Thai, Burmese, and even Vietnamese children, for whom Chinese is an even more foreign language than English; "Portuguese" speakers, upon further analysis, have been found to include speakers of Cape Verdean—a language considerably different from Portuguese; "French" speakers in New England may be speakers of Haitian creole or may come from long-established Franco American homes, and so on. Recognition of these rather gross differences as well as other more subtle distinctions can be critical to successful bilingual education programs.

Goal Setting

The bilingual community has to determine the objectives of the bilingual education program it wants to propose, the target population the program is to serve, and how this program will relate to the schools where it will be located. These issues are best defined by a coordinating committee of the type described earlier, with an organizational network that has the ability to disseminate these ideas to the bilingual community at large for its information and evaluation. Obviously, not everyone's opinion can be considered, but the members of the community should have the opportunity to learn what is happening and be aware that they can communicate their thoughts to the coordinating committee. The mass media can be most helpful; it would be a good idea to include on the coordinating committee any member of the bilingual community who works on a newspaper or magazine, or in TV or radio.

Each of the following issues will involve a choice of alternatives for the individual communities:

Objective. A bilingual program can seek to maintain the language and culture of a particular ethnic-linguistic group or groups; it can serve as a bridge to bring children into the monolingual English educational system; it can be used to revive a disappearing language.

Target Population. A bilingual program can be developed to serve non-English-speaking children or those with limited abilities; it can be directed toward all children of an ethnic minority as well as other children interested in learning the language and culture of that group.

Relation to School. A bilingual program can be separate or it can be integrated—to a variety of degrees—into the total curriculum of the school where it is located.

The choice of goal and target population will depend on the philosophy of the community, the characteristics of the children to be served, and the existing legislative constraints. In determining the relationship to the school, desegregation rulings will have to be considered. Once the alternatives have been agreed upon, the community can communicate them to the school board, superintendent, and monolingual teaching personnel. The process of negotiation, development, and implementation of the plan may be a long one. During the process, the initial plan will probably suffer changes. From the outset, one of the constant dilemmas is the choice between quantity and quality. Should a quality program for a few children be set up and then be expanded periodically until it serves all children? Or should a weaker program covering more children be established with the hope of gradual improvement? It is usually the case that mandated bilingual education forces school districts to provide services for as many children as possible.

Technical Issues

The bilingual community should also conduct research, discuss, and draw up its conclusions regarding type of language(s) to be included in the program, curriculum, materials, testing instruments and procedures, personnel qualifications, and resources. The more detailed the information the community can provide to the decision-making authorities, the more significant its contribution will be.

Language Type. The language other than English included in the program can be an international language with an extensive literature; it can be of limited use; or it may not have a written system. Depending upon this, the language may be used as a medium of instruction for all or some subjects. If the language is not written, it can either be used orally, or a writing system can be developed, which is a much more complex task.[7]

Curriculum. Decisions have to be made as to how the language will be taught, what language(s) will be used as a medium of instruction in the teaching of subject matter, what subject matter will be included, and how the culture of the children is going to be reflected in the curriculum.[8]

Materials. Materials can be commercially produced, developed at special centers, or teacher-developed. Availability and type of language and curriculum will influence decisions on materials. Materials should be evaluated for quality and for language and content level.[9]

Testing Instruments and Procedures. Tests can be used to determine placement or progress and, in certain types of programs, to ascertain eligibility for and completion of the program. It is important to locate appropriate instruments and to ensure that the personnel administering these tests are qualified to do so. The issue of testing is particularly important, because some of the most crucial decisions in the program are based on test results.[10]

Personnel Qualifications. Teachers and other personnel should be qualified in their particular field or subject area and should also have a degree of fluency in English and another language; they should know about first and second language acquisition and acquisition of reading and writing skills; they should be acquainted with the behavior patterns, value systems, and cognitive styles of the two cultures; they should know what methods, curricula, materials, and tests are applicable to the bilingual situation; and they should know how to work with parents of bilingual children. Teacher preparation will have to be inservice in most cases, until there are enough graduates of recently begun teacher-training programs to fill the positions available. Waiver systems have been used in some cases where qualified personnel lacked certification.[11]

Bilingual programs are already in operation in many communities. A survey and evaluation of these programs should be the first step toward solving some of these technical problems. The bilingual community should also make an inventory of its available human resources with regard to language ability, professional background, and possible role in the program (with or without further training). Community agencies can be most helpful in gathering this type of information. This strategy helps to prevent charges of inability to start a program due to lack of personnel and to avoid unfair hiring practices.

The tasks described in the three preceding sections are too numerous and complex for any one small group of individuals to undertake. All of the various components of the bilingual community should assume specific roles, since functional specialization can produce better results. Bilingual teachers and parents are most suited to reach other parents to collect information and provide feedback during the various stages of the planning. Bilingual school personnel can help obtain information on the current school situation, the needs of the children, and—if there is already some bilingual education—which educational strategies seem to work best and which materials and tests seem most appropriate. Professionals and bilingual experts associated with universities and planning agencies can provide results of research and whatever information that is applicable to the particular situation. They can also assist in the dissemination of information by teaching persons who have direct access to the parents about the rationale and basis for bilingual education. They can also cooperate in interpreting the data collected on the children, curriculum design, and selection of materials and tests. Universities can further cooperate by developing teacher-training programs.

Program Development

School districts often find themselves at a loss when they are required to start or expand bilingual education programs. A number of questions immediately arise: What kind of program? Where do we find teachers and materials? How many and which children should be included? The community should take advantage of this situation and propose their own plan based on the data collected and decisions made during the preparatory stages. This procedure has several advantages: the usual delays caused by needs assessments and planning procedures having to be conducted by school officials with little or no experience in bilingual education can be avoided, and the community will be ensured of participation in the choice of curricula, materials, personnel, and other elements of the program. For this to happen, however, it is crucial for the community to be prepared and to have established working relationships with the school system.

Two other important issues to consider in the early stages of implementation of a program are the hiring of bilingual personnel and the scope of the school budget. The bilingual community should ensure that the bilingual personnel are hired under the same conditions as other school personnel and not—as is frequently the case—on temporary assignments that deprive them of job security and benefits. The community should also understand the school budget. The bilingual community must stress the point that bilingual children are part of the permanent population of the school district, which is responsible for their education. Consequently, funds for the education of these children should be furnished through the school budget rather than only through federal assistance or additional funds.

The community's interest should not subside when a bilingual education program takes effect. What has been agreed upon on paper does not always become a reality. Therefore, it is important to monitor the development of the program. Representatives involved earlier in the planning stages may now play significant roles as monitors of progress. It is important that the monitoring representatives have the trust of the entire community and that their role be perceived in this way by all parties concerned. They should establish a relationship with the school district which will allow them to influence as well as monitor the implementation of the plan agreed upon.

Summary and Conclusions

One often hears of Coral Way, Rough Rock, and the Oyster School as examples of quality bilingual education. The initiation of these programs was preceded by long-term planning on the part of the community and interested school personnel and long-term negotiating with school authorities. At present, the process is very different. Schools have received mandates to implement bilingual education programs, and lawyers and community groups are forced to deliver a program—all under extreme time constraints. The author has worked with communities where decisions were made which seemed best under the circumstances, but there was not enough time to consider the long-term consequences. Since legislation is based on precedent, the effect of those decisions will be felt by many other communities going through similar processes. Consequently, on the basis of the experience of the "model programs," it is proposed that communities start planning immediately in order to be ready for a mandate, rather than start developing a plan after the order has come.

Another important issue is the composition of the bilingual community. Increasing numbers of members of linguistic minorities are being trained in various careers. Recruiting them as part of the "community" alongside "grass roots" members is crucial if positive results are to be attained in exercising pressure.

The concept of members of minority groups' improving their education and social status without forgetting their community origins is no longer unrealistic. Ethnicity is becoming a source of political power. Membership in a particular ethnic group crosses socioeconomic boundaries. Having technical assistance furnished by members of the community provides—in addition to the more tangible effects—role models for its younger members and enhances their pride in their heritage.

Because of budgetary, personnel, and other constraints, the community will have to set priorities in developing a bilingual program. The long-term plan, however, should include *all* of the components that could possibly contribute to its success and should reach all the children for whom it will be a better form of education. It is better to start on a small scale and plan gradual growth and improvement than to accept a better-than-nothing type of program of dubious quality. The best defense for the concept of bilingual education is successful bilingual education.

Notes

[1]Some examples are Coral Way, Florida; Rough Rock, Arizona; San Antonio Unified School District, Texas; and the Oyster School, Washington, D.C. See Patricia L. Engle, *The Use of Vernacular Languages in Education,* Papers in Applied Linguistics: Bilingual Education Series (Arlington, Va.: Center for Applied Linguistics, 1975); Vera P. John and Vivian M. Horner, *Early Childhood Bilingual Education* (New York: Modern Language Association, 1971); and Luis Ortega, *Introduction to Bilingual Education* (New York: Anaya-Las Américas, 1975).

[2]See Hannah N. Geffert et al., *The Current Status of U.S. Bilingual Education Legislation,* Papers in Applied Linguistics: Bilingual Education Series (Arlington, Va.: Center for Applied Linguistics, 1975) and Series on Languages and Linguistics (Arlington, Va.: ERIC Clearinghouse on Languages and Linguistics, 1975) ED 107 135; and Center for Law and Education, *Bilingual-Bicultural Education: A Handbook for Attorneys and Community Workers* (Cambridge, Mass.: CLE, 1975).

[3]For alternatives, see José Cárdenas, "Bilingual Education, Segregation, and a Third Alternative," *Inequality of Education* 19 (February, 1975): 19-22.

[4]The two major firms are the Puerto Rican Legal Defense Fund and the Mexican American Legal Defense Fund. Local legal assistance offices also take up cases, sometimes with the cooperation of one of the major firms.

[5]Anthony F. Panzetta, "The Concept of Community: The Short-circuit of the Mental Health Movement," in Kramer and Specht, eds., *Readings in Community Organization Practice* (Englewood Cliffs, N.J.: Prentice-Hall, Inc., 1975), p. 28.

[6]Alan E. Guskin and Robert Ross, "Advocacy and Democracy: The Long View," in Fred M. Cox et al., eds., *Strategies of Community Organization* (Itasca, Ill.: F.E. Peacock, 1974), p. 340.

[7]There are at present Title VII bilingual programs in more than forty languages. Many more are locally or privately funded.

[8]For descriptions of different types of bilingual programs see Theodore Andersson and Mildred Boyer, *Bilingual Schooling in the United States,* 2 vols. (Washington, D.C.: U.S. Government Printing Office, 1970) ED 039 527; Andrew D. Cohen, *A Sociolinguistic Approach to Bilingual Education* (Rowley, Mass.: Newbury House, 1975); P. Engle (see note 1); W.E. Lambert and G.R. Tucker, *Bilingual Education of Children: The St. Lambert Experiment* (Rowley, Mass.: Newbury House, 1972), ED 082 573; William F. Mackey, *Bilingual Education in a Binational School* (Rowley, Mass.: Newbury House, 1972); Manuel

Ramírez, III, et al., *Spanish-English Bilingual Education in the U.S.: Current Issues, Resources, and Research Priorities*, Papers in Applied Linguistics, 1977) and Series on Languages and Linguistics (Arlington, Va.: ERIC Clearinghouse on Languages and Linguistics, 1977), FL 088 272; and the *Project Information Packages* prepared by the Office of Education and available from the Bilingual Education Office of the Office of Education.

[9]The Bilingual Education Office (Title VII, ESEA) of the Office of Education has funded a network of resource, material, and dissemination centers that can provide information on curriculum, materials, and tests. For further sources see M. Ramírez, note 8.

[10]Two Title VII Dissemination Centers (Cambridge, Massachusetts, and Austin, Texas) are collecting information on tests. Some other work has been or is being done at Hunter College, Berkeley, Columbia University, and other institutions of higher education. See also Ramírez, note 8.

[11]Throughout the country a large number of teacher-training programs have been funded through Title VII. These programs can provide information on teacher qualifications. See also Center for Applied Linguistics, *Guidelines for the Preparation and Certification of Teachers of Bilingual/Bicultural Education in the United States of America*, 1974, ED 098 809.

The Chicago Parent Leadership Training Program

María B. Cerda and Jean J. Schensul

There is general consensus among educators that parental involvement *is* and *must continue to be* an integral part of bilingual education. This consensus is supported by federal guidelines for bilingual education programs, by state mandates, and by local board of education policies. But although the advisability of involving parents in educational issues is widely recognized, in many cases recognition of the concept has generated little else beyond a great deal of talk.

The Chicago Latino Institute philosophy dictates that other actions are needed, in addition to legislation, policies, and well-wishing, if parental involvement is to become a reality. A systematic approach to the provision of resources to develop involvement is essential if parents are to become effective participants in the process of educating their children.

Bilingual education is more than just a school program impacting children in classrooms; it has the promise of providing a complete educational environment not limited to, or contained within, the walls of classrooms, but reaching out and incorporating the resources of the total community.

Based on this concept, the Latino Institute organized a three-year Parent Leadership Training Program with the overall goal of developing leadership among Latino parents whose children were enrolled in the bilingual programs offered by the Chicago Public School System.

In the following pages, we will describe the experiences, including the pitfalls, encountered by the Latino Institute trainers as they progressed from their own basic training to implementing the first program of its type for parental involvement in bilingual education in Chicago. In order to convey a bit of the unique local Chicago flavor, we will start with a brief history of Latinos in the city.

Background

Chicago's Latino community is very diverse. While the majority of the population consists of persons of Mexican and Puerto Rican origin or descent, other Latin American groups are represented in increasingly large numbers. Historically, there has been a lack of communication among these various nationalities, a fact which has had negative implications for the Latino community in general. The single overriding issue of historical and current importance which brings parents and community representatives together from all sectors and nationalities within the Latino community of Chicago is education. Latinos view education as the most important area offering the possibility of upward mobility to children and young adults, and bilingual education is providing the needed services to increase this mobility. Thus education, particularly bilingual education, was seen by the Latino Institute as offering the greatest potential for bringing Latinos together around a common goal.

The Latino communities had been advocating bilingual education since the late 1960s. State and federally funded bilingual programs in Chicago were mandated to have functioning advisory councils participating in the planning and implementation of bilingual programs, but the gap in educational leadership on a citywide, as well as local, level was a serious problem in view of the projected transfer of bilingual education funds from federal and state to city Board of Education sources. This transfer and the continuity of bilingual education was considered to require extensive ongoing support by parents, as well as by community organizations and advocacy groups.

Article 14 of the Illinois State Bilingual Act requires formation of bilingual councils consisting of parents and other community members for the planning, implementation, and coordination of the state mandated bilingual programs. The Parent Leadership Training Program, then, was specifically designed to facilitate the development of fully functional bilingual councils that would relate to the education of the Latino community in Chicago. Through training in reality-oriented issues and concerns, the participation of parents in the schools and in the decision-making processes of educational policies affecting their children and their communities would be maximized. Thus, the Parent Leadership Training Program, funded by the Rockefeller Foundation, was commenced in July 1975.

Phase I, 1975-1976: The Pilot Program

The first year of the Parent Leadership Training Program was directed toward staff development in the field, program development, and the creation of a series of training strategies and curriculum materials. The specific objectives of the first year were the following:

1. To train and develop a cadre of five trainers who would (a) be informed about bilingual education, Latino communities in Chicago, Chicago's public education system, and training processes and (b) be able to work as a team to facilitate the development of members of bilingual program advisory councils

2. To develop a pilot training program, including the development

of curricula, procedures for entering and phasing out of schools, and procedures for evaluating ongoing intervention efforts

3. To develop twenty fully functioning bilingual bicultural advisory councils (BBACs)

After a careful screening process, five trainers were hired from Latino communities throughout Chicago. These trainers represented a cross section of the citywide Latino population in terms of nationality, age, and experience in community and educational settings. Most of the trainers were relatively young, in contrast to the parents whom they were to train; two of the trainers were Puerto Rican, and three were Mexican American. It has been said that parents can only be trained by their peers. The training group was selected specifically to test whether a group of young Latinos of mixed nationalities could effectively train mainly older Puerto Rican and Mexican American parents.

During the summer of 1975, trainers underwent an intensive three-month period of training in group process skills, the politics and processes of education in the Chicago public schools, bilingual education, self-awareness, ethnic and national identity, and community characteristics. This group began work with the schools and bilingual advisory councils during the late fall of 1975.

Before the initiation of the training program, the administration of the Institute made a policy decision to work through, rather than outside, the public education system. This decision was made because it was felt that only by working through the system could school personnel be made to understand that parents have a role to play in bilingual program policy and classroom process. The Latino Institute administration was acutely aware of the way in which educators frequently give lip service to parental involvement. The training program wished to demonstrate, through its presence in the schools, that parents could contribute, but only if resources were made available to enhance their capabilities and develop their potential through a well thought-out program.

To facilitate training in the field, as well as to develop a pilot training model, work during the first year was focused on long-range training in individual schools across the city. In this first year work in the field was accompanied by a rigorous inservice program. This ongoing effort involved weekly case review by school, the development of group and individual problem-solving skills, and the resolution of internal staff conflicts caused by differences in approach. Trainers found this procedure extremely important in team building and skills development. In addition, it generated a great deal of case data on individual schools and training strategies. Schools were selected initially for their large Latino student population and because their advisory councils appeared to be somewhat organized, thus offering a potential-

ly supportive training base. Once sites were located, existing knowledge of these schools, their staff, and the service community was
made available to the training component. Thus, when trainers
entered a school, they had considerable overall information about the
bilingual program, the local population, the district's educational
policy, and the general features of the school. What was missing
during this early phase of development was detailed and current information about the sites, obtainable only through a more direct and
ongoing research process. More current information would have
allowed the trainer to avoid certain actions and plan more effectively.
A more thorough on-site research process was incorporated into the
following year's activities.

In the field, trainers worked in teams of two or more, sharing responsibilities across sites, and gaining exposure to various aspects of
training in a number of different situations. This manner of organizing
the training program permitted trainers to obtain a wide variety of experiences and welded them into a team able to plan creatively and implement training collaboratively. The training process included the
following:

1. **Research**
    a. Socioeconomic/political aspects of the community
    b. Local organizations
    c. Educational systems in the school and district
    d. Bilingual education in the school and district
    e. History of parent involvement
    f. Characteristics of the target population
    g. Key individuals active in bilingual education and/or parent
        participation
    h. Current school and district issues

2. **Entry Process in Schools Selected for Training** (contacting school
    officials in order to impart a clear understanding of the Parent
    Leadership Training Program)
    a. Contacting General Superintendent of Chicago Public Schools
    b. Contacting district superintendents
    c. Contacting school principals
    d. Meeting with BBAC officers
    e. Attending BBAC meetings
    f. Interviewing BBAC members and parents with children in
        the bilingual program

3. **Orientation**
    a. Arranging for presentation to potential participants at
        BBAC or other scheduled meetings

     b.   Setting time, date, and place of first session

     c.   Inviting parents to participate and having them sign attendance sheets

4. **Needs Assessment**

     a.   Beginning to establish rapport among parents and between parents and trainers

     b.   Determining group needs, priorities, and concerns related to information and skills development

     c.   Beginning to identify possible topics for future sessions

5. **Development of Training Plan**

     a.   Determining content priorities

     b.   Setting training objectives

     c.   Selecting and developing methods and handouts

     d.   Presenting training objectives and content to potential participants for their input and approval

     e.   Finalizing time lines and length of training

6. **Implementation**

     a.   Identifying staff persons to coordinate and implement training plan

     b.   Identifying and contacting resource persons in the community, school system, organizations, and training groups who could help in the implementation of the training plan

     c.   Arranging for regularly scheduled sessions with participants and establishing mechanisms for contacting them periodically

     d.   Preparing lesson plans for each session which included an evaluation section

7. **Evaluation**

     a.   Writing reports on the results of each session which included the feedback and evaluation of participants

     b.   Asking for evaluative feedback from other resource persons present at the session

     c.   Receiving evaluation of entire training process and content as well as trainer's performance from cotrainers, session trainers, and/or training supervisor

     d.   Writing a final report at the conclusion of training intervention, including a review of the entire process from research phase to evaluation

     e.   Documenting in the final report recommendations for improving future training interventions with each group and/or school, including suggestions for follow-up

8. **Follow-up**
   a. Contacting administrators and obtaining their approval of the training aims
   b. Conducting update on relevant information previously researched
   c. Meeting with potential participants to reorient them and to determine current training needs
   d. Developing follow-up training plan
   e. Evaluating and making recommendations

Although there are a variety of training interventions designed for the Parent Leadership Training Program, only one intervention was utilized during the first year: long-range training, eight to twelve weeks per school.

This type of intervention utilized the entire basic curriculum of the Parent Leadership Training Program to develop members of bilingual advisory councils into a smoothly functioning group willing to plan activities and address issues in their own school context, and likely to maintain continuity for a period of years.

The long-range training process included the eight steps listed above, while the long-range training curriculum included the following:

1. Group and leadership identity
2. Decision-making processes
3. The roles and responsibilities of parents and BBACs in bilingual education, including the function of the executive committee
4. Various aspects of bilingual education on national, state, and local levels
5. Strategies for planning, setting goals and objectives, problem solving, and assessing accomplishments
6. Specific topics such as desegregation, parent observation in school and classroom, and how to expand a BBAC

These and other areas were communicated through a variety of training methods including lecturettes, pull learning, brain-storming sessions, informal incorporation of information into discussions, team planning, role playing, charts, handouts, personal awareness techniques, and simulations. Often, reality-based problems which the parents were interested in addressing formed the basis for the training process (and added motivation and immediacy).

The areas of the curriculum identified above and the training strategies are interchangeable and have been used in all of the intervention modes.

In addition, during the initial year, plans were developed and implemented for a district conference on bilingual education for parents, teachers, and administrators, which laid the basis for the district approach to be carried out the following year. Finally, a curriculum was developed which combined training techniques with information about bilingual advisory councils. The curriculum was relatively flexible in format and thus useful in a number of different training settings.

Training experiences during the first year illuminated the following problems:

1. Training on the individual school level was an inefficient way of using training resources (the number of bilingual programs doubled from 60 to 120 during the first year of our program due to implementation of the state mandate).

2. School-level training did not build links between schools on the district level and thus offered no way of institutionalizing BBAC leadership.

3. Parent turnover on the individual school level was considerable; some way was required to identify key potential leadership and concentrate some training with these individuals.

4. School BBAC situations were different: some schools required limited training; others required many sessions; and some were viewed as undesirable for training.

5. Trainers found a variety of situations which hindered training in local schools, situations which could have been predicted with sufficient knowledge of the setting.

6. The organization of the training group was suitable for training trainers, but not for training parents; responsibilities needed to be divided differently to maximize training time.

7. Schools were linked to communities; some way had to be found to build on those links rather than to view the schools as isolated organizations.

Responses to this set of problems included the following:

1. A research process was developed in which trainers spent several months researching school districts and individual schools to maximize the selection of training groups for potential impact.

2. Schools and key parents with leadership promise were identified through either research or a district conference. Training then proceeded, first on the district level, then on the local school level.

3. It was decided to train only executive members of the BBACs

rather than all parents, in order to avoid the problem of parent turnover or lack of continuing interest and commitment.

4. A differentiated approach to training on the local level was implemented; schools received "tailor made" training plans determined by needs assessments. (While the needs assessment approach was implemented during the first year, it became far more sophisticated during the second.)

5. Teams were paired by district and task, allowing for concentrated effort by trainers in individual districts, as well as for clear-cut overall task differentiation for monitoring and supervisory purposes.

Phase II, 1976-1977: Full Training Cycle

The second phase of the training program was marked by a more selective approach to training and an attempt, through district-level training and careful identification of long-range training sites, to intensify impact on the local level. The programmatic objectives for the second phase included the following:

1. To facilitate the linking of key parents, teachers, organizations, and other individuals by providing the environment for dialogue and the organizational framework for the effective functioning of the bilingual education system

2. To facilitate the development of ten fully functional bilingual councils, through the Parent Leadership Training Program, that would deal on an ongoing basis with issues and situations related to the education of the Latino community in Chicago

3. To test intervention strategies

Approaches to training included the following:

1. Specialized training for members of BBAC executive committees on the district level

2. Long-range training to meet the information and problem solving needs of more advanced groups on the local level

3. Short-range training to meet the informational and problem-solving needs of more advanced groups on the local level

4. Follow-up training to provide some assistance and information to groups which had received long-range training the previous year

5. Intensive training offered on a citywide basis to key parents who showed potential for further leadership training

6. District conferences to disseminate information and identify key parents in districts or groups of districts

Site reviews at the end of the second year revealed some interesting patterns of leadership development and new directions for implementation. These patterns included the following:

1. Training sessions tended to attract a relatively small core of parents from which BBAC leadership tended to emerge.

2. The presidents of BBACs sometimes entered the group "from the outside" rather than through the training process; other members of the executive team usually were from the training group.

3. Presidents of BBACs often dominated rather than facilitated the group process. This tended to result in concrete accomplishments in relation to the group and the school but, since leadership depended on these individuals who were sometimes transient, the continuity of the group was threatened.

4. The training group and BBACs often became interested in a range of other issues besides bilingual education.

5. A number of training group members were elected, through planning facilitated on the local level by the training program, to district and citywide advisory councils.

The second year of the Parent Leadership Training Program, then, contained the seeds of a broader, multifaceted approach to leadership training through community education.

Phase III, 1977-78: Institutionalization

The major thrust of the third year was on institutionalization through follow-up in districts in which specialized and long-range training had taken place the previous year. The intention of the third-year follow-up was to consolidate training of key parents, including executive members and other interested persons, through the provision of additional information and problem-solving skills. Key parents were included in cluster follow-up training on the district level as a way of dealing with extensive parent turnover in the executive group. In addition, an effort was made in some districts to develop a districtwide parent network.

While follow-up was the primary activity of the third year, trainers also planned and implemented a number of district conferences, teacher inservice activities, and orientation presentations to parent groups on parental involvement in bilingual education. In addition, they trained CETA (Comprehensive Employment and Training Act) personnel to become trainer aides.

District conferences were originally designed to disseminate information about district support for bilingual education, the identity of key resource persons and parent and community activists, issues and problems in education affecting Latino children, and the overall status of bilingual advisory council development. During the second and third years of the program, conferences were held in eleven districts. The process of developing district conferences was time-consuming. For this reason, the original notion of the conference as a lead-in to training on the district level was found to be less useful than anticipated. The conferences came to be used as vehicles for disseminating information and helping to facilitate the linking of key parents, community members, and school officials. Conferences also provided the environment for dialogue and the organizational framework to deal with the latest issues concerning the Latino community. The conference format usually involved contacting school and community representatives in bilingual education or advisory councils on the district and local school levels. Usually a district or multi-district planning group was formed to take on the responsibility for the conference, facilitated by a team of training program staff persons.

Intensive training offered a three-day training institute to parents, identified on a citywide basis, who showed interest and strong leadership potential during the second year of training. The intensive training intervention was designed to further reinforce the knowledge and skills of these parents so that they would be more likely to facilitate the development of the BBACs with which they were affiliated.

Trainers also wanted the opportunity to test the trainer's manual, developed through the training staff inservice program. Variations of the intensive training mode were utilized in several school sites.

During the third year, the Institute began to seek CETA funds to train a group of parents to assist trainers as "trainer aides." This effort was also designed as an inservice opportunity for both experienced and new training staff.

The CETA program training content included the following areas:

1. Bilingual education, desegregation, and other aspects of education affecting Latino children in Chicago

2. Participatory techniques and methods for learning

3. Basic group issues and how to work more effectively with groups

4. Problem solving; research techniques; communication; decision making; organizing techniques, such as developing networks of communication between parents; leadership styles; etc.

These parents were expected to help other parents or groups of parents by providing information on bilingual education, serving as resource persons at community gatherings, acting as effective group members in advisory councils, organizing bilingual committees, negotiating with schools, etc. With their knowledge and skills, the trainer aides would serve as a support and moving force for parents in addressing issues of bilingual education in the city. These parents were selected for their display of leadership potential. Many of them are currently active in district or citywide advisory groups as well as on the local level. They will increase the effective service of the training program significantly, and their community involvement will offer important input into new programmatic thrusts.

In order to facilitate the formation of a sound bilingual education program, communication and collaboration between parents and teachers are mandatory. The first-year experience in pilot schools suggested that both parents and teachers were seeking ways of effectively involving parents in the classroom and in the school. In response to this need, training workshops were developed to identify strategies for parent-teacher collaboration. These workshops, intended mainly for teachers, encouraged participants to explore areas of resistance to parental involvement and to plan ways of drawing on the strengths of parents both in the classroom and at home. They also stressed to teachers the importance of acquiring greater familiarity with the communities in which they were teaching to increase understanding of the parent perspective.

Parents were not included in these teacher workshops because it had been the experience of the trainers that when parents and teachers participated in the same program, workshop, or committee, parents tended to be intimidated and did not express their opinions, ask questions, nor make the important contributions offered in other settings. Thus, as parents had been trained separately, so it was the design of the training component to train teachers separately, in a dialogical model. In the future, when both groups are able to meet with each other independently, with their responsibilities and directions clear, the training component will facilitate joint training sessions.

The major areas of concern which emerged as a result of the last assessment were the following:

1. The need to develop flexible formats which integrated training with emphasis on "real life" problems or events, rather than on "out of context" teaching strategies which participants were expected to translate into actual situations.

2. The need to develop reasonable, viable research in conjunction with training in order to enhance the training capabilities. The training component never had the resources to do effective research on programmatic issues.

3. The need to move beyond education and into other related areas of community development and leadership training, both to

meet the needs of parents and to meet the broader needs of Latino communities of Chicago.

Summary

In summary, the program has supported the organization and development of at least forty bilingual advisory groups and their executives, facilitated the election of thirty-four parents to district and citywide advisory positions, influenced city and statewide legislation and implementation of bilingual programs, and disseminated information on bilingual education and related issues to many hundreds of parents over the course of the past three years.

Over and above its impact at the local school and district level, the Parent Leadership Training Program has become known and influential in the Chicago area, regionally, and nationally. The Institute is called upon to develop training curricula, to run training sessions, to serve as an advocate for bilingual education, and to facilitate the development and implementation of overall advocacy strategies. Members of the training program, and trainees from the various citywide and local training groups, have run sessions and workshops and offered presentations at national conferences in bilingual education, anthropology, and multicultural education and parent involvement.

Prior to the Chicago bilingual mandate and the Office of Civil Rights plan of 1976, there was virtually no parental involvement of significance in bilingual education in Chicago, despite state and federal legislation. Bilingual advisory councils were token in nature, with officers usually appointed by parent or bilingual coordinators or the principal, to comply with the law but not with the spirit of the law.

During the first year of the training program, training staff worked closely with the Office of Civil Rights plan for bilingual education. Members assisted in establishing goals, objectives, and bylaws concerning parent involvement and training. As a result of this work, and the advocacy stance of the Institute in relation to leadership training in bilingual education, the following changes have taken place in the system:

1. The public schools have institutionalized the training of parents for involvement in advisory committees and have allocated resources for such training.

2. The city has hired a citywide parent coordinator and a number of training program trainees to support parental training in local schools and school districts.

3. The Bureau of Multilingual Education has instituted a citywide bilingual advisory council. Staff of the training program have been asked to help train this advisory council.

Generally, parents are now viewed by the Chicago public school system as important contributors to bilingual programs, and ways are being sought to train them and to incorporate them into classrooms and committees. This has made all our efforts worthwhile.

Parent/Community Involvement in the Mississippi Choctaw Bilingual Education Program

Kennith H. York

The issue of involving Indian parents and Indian communities in bilingual programs predominantly structured for other Americans has been a great concern for educators, anthropologists, linguists, and government officials. Getting Native American Indians enthused and excited about bilingual education as defined by the Congress of the United States has been one of the greatest challenges for most American Indian bilingual programs. The purpose of this paper is not to describe problems in involving Indian parents/communities in bilingual education programs, but to report on how one American Indian tribe, the Mississippi Choctaws, has attempted to involve Choctaw parents and Choctaw communities.

The Mississippi Band of Choctaw Indians

The Mississippi Band of Choctaw Indians is composed of approximately 3,700 Choctaw Indians located on or near seven reservation communities in east central Mississippi. Members of this tribe are the descendants of those Choctaws who refused to leave their homeland when the majority of the Choctaws were removed west of the Mississippi River during the "Trail of Tears" of the 1830s, 1840s, 1850s, and 1903. Living in an unfriendly macrosociety, the Choctaw Indians have retained their ethnic identity (well over 90 percent are classified as "fullbloods" by the Bureau of Indian Affairs) and native language (roughly 86 percent of the people speak Choctaw in their homes) by purposely not assimilating to any noticeable extent with the other races surrounding them. Since the removals the Mississippi Choctaws have lived as an isolated, poverty stricken, rural minority in the area which once belonged to the Choctaw Nation. Today the dominant population is composed of "Blacks" and "Whites."

In 1962, 84.7 percent of Choctaw households made less then $2,000 annual cash income, whereas, in 1968, only 34.8 percent of Choctaw households made less than $2,000.[1] Despite a slight increase in employment and income in the 1970s, the majority of the Mississippi Choctaw people are still below the poverty line since the average Choctaw household contains 5.5 members.

Choctaw Language

There are numerous dialects of Choctaw spoken in the seven communities today. These communities are patterned after traditional Choctaw villages or towns, and many have retained their traditional names. These are (1) Pearl River (Bihi Ayaša), (2) Tucker (Imokla Ayaša), (3) Standing Pine (Tiyak Hikiya), (4) Red Water (Oka Homma), (5) Big Creek (Bok Čito), (6) Silver-striped Skunk (Koni Hata), and (7) Red Creek (Bok Homma). There are also dialectical variations between the Choctaws in Mississippi and Oklahoma. However, a native speaker of the language does not have insurmountable problems with the language and with the dialects. The Chickasaw language is also closely related to Choctaw, and some linguists believe that the two tribes spoke the same language in times past.

The Choctaw language has had a written form for over 150 years. The school system developed by early missionaries and supported by the Choctaw Nation before the removals of the nineteenth century used textbooks printed in English and Choctaw. The "public" system which began in the neighborhood churches in the 1890s utilized a bilingual approach. Unfortunately, this practice did not continue when the Bureau of Indian Affairs initiated the present system in 1918-20. Furthermore, printed materials were taken to Oklahoma during the removals. When bilingual education came to the Choctaw schools in 1974, there was very little printed material in the Choctaw language; thus, the majority of the Mississippi Choctaw people were illiterate in their own language.

School System

The Bureau of Indian Affairs (BIA) school system operates elementary "neighborhood" schools in five of the seven reservation communities and a K-12 school in another. The remaining community, Bok Homma, is the smallest and most distant community and sends its children to a local public school. This BIA system has an enrollment of over 1,250 students and employs approximately 65 classroom teachers. Only a small percentage of these teachers are Mississippi Choctaws, and they are the only teachers who can speak the native language of the students. The opportunity to receive formal education is relatively new for the Mississippi Choctaws. The present system was set up in 1918-20, but a high school was not established until 1964. Prior to that time, very few Choctaws completed high school because of social (segregated Mississippi society) and economic reasons.

The six BIA schools range from the original frame school buildings constructed in 1920 to a modern elementary and high school complex. In terms of physical plant and equipment, the BIA schools rank among the best in the state of Mississippi.

Since the Choctaw communities are scattered, almost all Choctaw students are bused. However, boarding facilities are provided in the three largest Choctaw schools.

Prebilingual Education

The Mississippi Choctaws did not begin to reevaluate the BIA school system until 1967. During the era of community action programs, the Choctaw Tribe actively sought new programs which would meet the needs of children from Choctaw-speaking homes. Receiving a grant from the National Follow-Through Office, the tribal officials selected the Tucson Early Educational Model (TEEM) under the assumption that TEEM utilized a bilingual approach since the model had worked with Mexican American children in Arizona.[2] However, due to various factors, TEEM provided only an oral translation model with Choctaw paraprofessionals serving as translators. Bilingual bicultural emphasis in teacher education was not provided for the Choctaw staff in the Follow-Through Program.

After three years of TEEM, the Choctaw Tribal Council established the Choctaw Board of Education which had as its sole purpose to be the governing authority in Choctaw education. The CBE requested the Bureau of Indian Affairs to evaluate the entire Choctaw Indian Agency School System. The evaluation report *An Education Evaluation: The Choctaw and Chitimachi Schools* (1973), was prepared under the direction of Robert Rebert, who was an employee at the BIA Educational Resources Center in Albuquerque, New Mexico. One of the main recommendations made by Rebert et al. was the establishment of bilingual bicultural instruction for Choctaw children attending the Choctaw schools.[3] Using the evaluation report prepared by BIA, the Mississippi Choctaw Tribe submitted proposals to the Title VII Office of Bilingual Education.

Target Population

Almost all Choctaw children are fluent speakers of Choctaw when they enter school; the remainder, for the most part, comprehend Choctaw. Choctaw adults use the language in almost all community circumstances among themselves. The same is true for children, teenagers, and young adults. Most children speak little or no English when they enter school. Those who do not speak Choctaw upon entrance into the school system tend to fall to peer pressure and acquire Choctaw, usually at great expense to their English. Thus, Choctaw is considered to be the native language of the children. This has occurred despite the emphasis on English as the medium of instruction by the BIA system.

The exclusive use of English as the school language had several consequences:[4]

1. Because English was used as the medium of instruction, basic content areas (social studies, math, science, etc.) suffered, since the children had limited understanding of the teacher.

2. The pupils were not acquiring basic lexicon in Choctaw, i.e., the

names of birds, animals, trees, colors, numbers, and other areas of the native vocabulary.

3. Since Choctaw was not used in the classroom, a diglossic situation had arisen, which is defined in the formal-informal context. Many of the Choctaw people, especially the younger speakers, were virtually incapable of carrying on a discourse in the native language in formal situations, such as in public meetings, even when it was crucial that they do so. This type of diglossia is extremely harmful to community interaction.

4. Children failed to learn adequate English because of the unstructured way in which English was used in the classroom. English was not a subject, but was the medium of instruction. The general tendency was for the children to learn enough "phrase-book" English for them to get through the day. Considerable evidence showed that the grammatical structures of English were not used productively by the children.

Bilingual Education for the Choctaws of Mississippi

In July 1974 the Mississippi Band of Choctaw Indians was awarded a bilingual education grant under Title VII of the Elementary and Secondary Education Act. There were two major purposes of the grant: (1) to plan and develop a bilingual education basic program to be implemented in grades K-3 of the Choctaw schools by fall 1975 and (2) to provide assistance of tuition, books, fees, and stipends for twelve Choctaw students to pursue B.S. degrees in elementary education. Known as Bilingual Education for Choctaws of Mississippi (BECOM), this project has served as an exemplary program for other Native American Indian bilingual education efforts.

Rationale for Parent/Community Involvement in the Program

Probably, the first learning experience every child receives is from the parent and the home. The home environment is important in the development of the child's self-concept. Parents and others with whom the child comes in contact have a responsibility for helping a child feel worthy, loved, and wanted, and a contributing member of the family and society. The Choctaw child is taught to have pride in the Choctaw culture.

Parent Involvement Activities

An essential aspect of the Choctaw bilingual program is parent involvement. The value of strong parental support in developing an adequate educational program is recognized.

Choctaw parents serve on the Advisory Board for BECOM. Representatives from each of the communities make up the Advisory Board, which recommends changes in the program, provides community input into the administration, and formulates future direction and plans for the BECOM Program. Each representative must be a parent of a child or children receiving bilingual instruction in the Choctaw schools.

Other activities of Advisory Board members include orientation to bilingual education, review of duties and responsibilities, election of officers, and literacy training in the native language.

Some Choctaw parents serve as parent/community aides. The activities performed by parent aides vary, but they can be classified into three major areas:

A. *Demonstrations*   Qualified parents demonstrate or teach concepts or skills which relate to the Choctaw culture, e.g., weaving baskets, beading sashes, etc.

B. *Storytelling, Music, or Dance*   Parents come to the classrooms to tell stories from Choctaw folklore, teach Choctaw songs, and entertain the children with Choctaw music and dances.

C. *Special Events and Activities*   Parents are requested to assist in school learning experiences. The children are urged to bring their parents to school when there are special activities which include both Choctaw and non-Choctaw cultural events.

Each Choctaw child is encouraged to take home some evidence of the bilingual learning experiences received at school, e.g., completed written exercises, creative writing, arts or crafts, school books. The Choctaw child and parent may review some concept being discussed in social studies, or the child may request help from family members in identifying Choctaw names of plants or insects for a science lesson or report.

In order to enhance parent involvement with instructional materials, community literacy programs have been instituted. It is important that the child's educational program be favorably accepted and reinforced at home. This in turn helps to improve the attitude and achievement of the child at school. The objectives of this aspect of the program are (1) to build rapport with the parents through adequate communication; (2) to help the parents of Choctaw children attending school, and other interested members of the Choctaw community, to understand the school curriculum; (3) to solicit their help in developing the instructional program; (4) to gain their support in implementing the program; (5) to clarify conflicting values and goals; and (6) to provide literacy training in the school orthography so that parents can tutor children in the native language.

Parent Involvement in Evaluation

During the past two school years, the Bureau of Indian Affairs school administrators have questioned the effectiveness and parental support of bilingual education in the Choctaw schools. As part of the overall evaluation of the program, parent questionnaires were administered to parents of children in kindergarten through third grades. The questionnaires were given to parents by the Choctaw-speaking aides during summer break. Responses indicated that most Choctaw parents feel that it is important for their children to learn both Choctaw and English languages. The results of the questionnaires were published in the local community newspaper to gain other parental support for bilingual education in the Choctaw schools.

Native American Writer's Workshop

During 1978 the Center for Applied Linguistics, American Indian Programs, funded a writer's workshop for the BECOM program. The workshop was conceived as a mechanism to train Choctaw staff, many of whom are parents, to write about their experiences and to combine the written experiences into Choctaw literature for the program. Most of the workshop was conducted in the Choctaw language. About twenty Choctaw staff participated in the first writer's workshop. A second writer's workshop was conducted to (1) continue skill development in writing Choctaw materials and (2) approach a creative writing stage for the majority of the participants.

In the two workshops, pictures or concrete items were utilized as support for beginning writing. Each person was asked to choose items or pictures and write about them. Everyone had an opportunity to share his/her writing, and the entire group gave critiques to improve the writing. Once the critiques had been provided, the writer was required to draw illustrations to further clarify the written material.

The responses to the two writer's workshops were positive. There were numerous comments to continue the workshops and to include an illustrator's workshop to increase the quality of the materials.

The BECOM Project has conducted follow-up sessions since the initial two workshops. Other workshops are being planned which will include reading, writing, and illustrating. It is the opinion of the staff and this writer that conducting writer's workshops in the native language, such as the Choctaw language, has a great potential for high impact on community involvement and for ensuring implementation of bilingual education for Choctaw Indians.

Conclusion

Almost all federally subsidized educational programs for minority populations require some involvement of parents and communities.

Involvement of Indian parents and Indian communities in bilingual education programs has to include emphasis on Indian culture and language. Most Indian parents have to feel comfortable about the program and have some basic understanding of the purpose to truly support bilingual education. Bilingual instruction often eliminates serious problems in conflicting values between the school and the home.

One of the unique characteristics of the Mississippi Choctaws has been their belief in true bilingual development utilizing both Choctaw and non-Choctaw cultures and languages. The Choctaw parents wish for their children not only to be educated, but to be educated Choctaws.

Notes

[1]John H. Peterson, Jr., *Socio-Economic Characteristics of the Mississippi Choctaw Indians*, Social Science Research Center Report 34 (State College, Miss.: Mississippi State University, 1970).

[2]James R. Richburg, "An Ethnographic Description of the Choctaw Follow-Through Program from 1968 to 1971" (Ph.D. diss., University of Georgia, 1972).

[3]Robert J. Rebert, Paul L. Sward, and David C. Young, *An Education Evaluation: The Choctaw and Chitimachi Schools*, Final Report, Research Report No. 23 (Albuquerque: Indian Education Resources Center, 1973), p. 52.

[4]*Bilingual Education for the Choctaws of Mississippi (BECOM): Project Proposal, 1975-76*, submitted to USOE, Title VII, Office of Bilingual Education, p. 3.

Parent Advisory Councils Serving Spanish-English Bilingual Projects Funded under ESEA Title VII

Norberto Cruz, Jr.

Bilingual education funded under ESEA Title VII provides for parent and community involvement in all aspects of program planning, implementation, and evaluation. Parent advisory councils have been the vehicles for this involvement in bilingual programs. A year-long research project identifying roles and functions of parent advisory councils serving Spanish-English bilingual projects funded under ESEA Title VII was recently completed by the author of this paper. From the literature reviewed in preparation for the study, it was evident that roles and functions of parent advisory councils serving bilingual projects funded under ESEA Title VII have not been adequately specified nor have all the rules and regulations been strictly followed by some local education agencies receiving Title VII monies.

In the Bilingual Education Act of 1968, there was no language which mandated parent/community participation through an advisory council, committee, or other group. It did, however, state:

> Applications for grants. . . may be approved by the Commissioner only if. . . the program set forth in the application is consistent, with criteria established by the Commissioner. . . [1]

This provision gave the Commissioner the right to develop criteria which local and state educational agencies were required to meet in order to qualify for Title VII funds. In 1971 criteria for eligibility of Title VII funds were printed in the *Manual for Project Applicants and Grantees.*

The *Manual* stated:

> A project advisory group which consists of parents and community representatives should be formed before the project proposed is prepared and should continue to be involved at all stages of the project's development and operation.[2]

The *Manual* did not mandate parent advisory councils, which is evident by the word "should"; such wording was a suggestion rather than a regulation.

In May of 1974, hearings were held in Washington. D.C., and in New York City before the General Subcommittee on Education of the Committee on Education and Labor. Hearings were held on H.R. 1085, H.R. 2490, and H.R. 11464 which were bills proposed to amend ESEA Title VII. The testimony at the hearings revealed the importance of parent/ community involvement in bilingual programs. Recommendations for revisions of regulations by the National Advisory Committee on the Education of Bilingual Children reflected the views of witnesses giving testimony, as well as the views of committee members. The recommendation on advisory groups read as follows:

> . . . referring to advisory groups the word *may* be changed to *shall* and that the words *and others* be added after secondary school students.[3]

The Bilingual Education Act of 1974, in part because of recommendations by the National Advisory Committee on the Education of Bilingual Children, mandated participation by parents of children enrolled in bilingual programs. Specifically, the law read as follows:

> An application for a program of bilingual education shall be developed in consultation with parents of children of limited English-speaking ability, teachers, and, where applicable, secondary school students, in the areas to be served, and assurances shall be given in the application that, after the application has been approved under this title, the applicant will provide for participation by a committee composed of, and selected by, such parents and, in the case of secondary schools, representatives of secondary school students to be served.[4]

The Bilingual Education Act which now mandated parental involvement made it possible for new rules and regulations to be written for those agencies applying for Title VII funds. Rules and regulations which reflected the language of the new act were incorporated into the "Criteria for Governing Grants Awards" which appeared in the *Federal Register* on June 11, 1976.

Even with the legislation mandating participation by a "committee" (known as an "advisory group" in the rules and regulations), the quantity and quality of participation has been a concern to school officials and citizens. The functions of parent advisory councils vary from project to project, a fact revealed in a report entitled *Federal Programs Supporting Educational Change.* The report stated: "some councils' functions are purely ceremonial whereas others seem to actually contribute to policy."[5]

From a review of literature dealing with legislation and administrative policies on parent advisory councils in bilingual education programs, it is evident that a true lack of direction for the advisory council exists. Functions mentioned in the 1971 *Manual for Applicants and Grantees* were recommended guidelines and not mandated. In 1976, the *Federal Register* included "Criteria for Governing Grants Awards" for bilingual programs, which now required parental involvement, but there still existed a lack of precise direction with respect to the roles and functions of the parent advisory councils serving bilingual education.

It is assumed that if parent advisory councils in bilingual education are to function properly and to contribute to the program, roles and functions of the councils should be clearly defined in order for all parties to adequately fulfill their respective responsibilities. The author, being aware of the lack of direction for advisory councils, decided to do research with respect to roles and functions of advisory councils on bilingual education. The research study was a dissertation entitled "An Investigation of the Roles and Functions of Parent Advisory Councils Serving Spanish-English Bilingual Projects Funded under ESEA Title VII." The research was started in September 1976 and completed in June 1978.

The author's primary purpose in the study was to identify and examine the roles and functions of parent advisory councils in bilingual education programs. In order to accomplish this purpose, it seemed appropriate to investigate the perceptions of project directors, school principals, and parent advisory council chairpersons regarding the operation of advisory councils. Twenty-one Spanish-English bilingual projects funded under Title VII were randomly selected for the study. A project director, principal, and advisory council chairperson from each of the twenty-one projects were chosen to be participants in the nationwide research study. The aforementioned participants were chosen for the study because of their working relationship with the parent advisory council.

After an extensive review of literature, four roles were identified for councils: *advisor*, *supporter*, *director*, and *nonsupporter*. The four roles were defined for the participants in the research as follows:

Advisor: the council assists school officials by making recommendations concerning the total bilingual program

Supporter: the council interprets the program to the community and gives support to the goals and objectives developed by school officials

Director: the council has an influential role in formulating policy and actively solicits community support for or against proposed or existing policies

Nonsupporter: the council reacts against the bilingual program and does not support decisions made by school officials

Various functions were also identified under the three program areas of planning, implementation, and evaluation.

Program planning: textbook selection, course selection, budget planning, development of objectives, identification of needs, and planning of school facilities

Program implementation: identification of community resources and public relations, interpretation of the bilingual program to the community, curriculum support, personnel policies, and in-service training

Program evaluation: evaluation of students, teachers, administrators, program, parent advisory council, community, and objectives

The role and function descriptors were incorporated into a questionnaire in which the participants were asked to rank the roles and functions under each program area according to primacy. The sixty-three participants surveyed in the research study were also asked to answer questions concerning the organizational format, procedures, and composition of the advisory councils they represented. Responses were received from 67 percent of the chairpersons, 71 percent of the principals, and 95 percent of the project directors. Combined responses from the three groups of participants equaled 77 percent.

The study revealed that parent advisory councils serving Spanish-English bilingual projects were similar to advisory councils described by the literature with respect to: the organizational format of councils; the method of choosing chairpersons; the time, place, and frequency of meetings; the term of membership; and the method of making decisions. The majority of councils represented had organizational formats with rules that were either written or understood. Chairpersons were generally elected by the entire council. The majority of councils had meetings in the schools, once a month and in the evenings when the rate of attendance is higher. A one-year term of membership was specified in 65.3 percent of all responses. The method of making decisions by simple majority (51 percent) was the most prevalent, according to the responses received. The major differences relating to the mechanics of organization in councils were how the general membership was chosen and the number of members on a council. The literature indicated that general membership is most often attained by an election; however, in the councils surveyed in this study, general membership was most often achieved by volunteering one's services. The councils represented were composed of ten to fifteen or more than twenty members, which differs slightly from the recommended number of fifteen to twenty members.

It was evident from the data analyzed that there existed significant agreement within each group of chairpersons, principals, and project directors in regard to the ranking by importance of the roles and functions of parent advisory councils. The analysis of the data indicated that the role of advisor was ranked first, followed by the roles of supporter, director, and nonsupporter, in that sequence. Identification of needs and development of objectives were ranked first and second, respectively, in the program area of planning. Under the program area of implementation, interpretation of the program and public relations were ranked first and second, respectively. Under the third area of program evaluation, the respondents ranked evaluation of the bilingual program first and the evaluation of its objectives second.

The following conclusions from the study are based on several activities or situations which are not desirable and probably have a negative effect on bilingual programs. Over one-third of the respondents indicated that the board of education or the superintendent had not developed a formal plan or statement giving recognition to the council. Also, over half of the respondents stated that limits of authority were not specified by either the board of education or the superintendent. It is not known why most of the councils represented did not have the formal recognition of the board or the superintendent. With respect to limits of authority, an advisory council needs to be cognizant of what it can do and also know the acceptable procedures for successful accomplishment of duties. The literature reviewed for this study was explicit in regard to the limits of authority by emphasizing that councils were more efficient when limits were specified.

The instances of noncompliance by some councils not having at least half of the membership comprised of parents with children enrolled in the bilingual program were very small, with only 6.1 percent of the respondents indicating this to be the situation in the councils they represented. However, the instances of noncompliance by some councils not existing prior to the preparation of the proposal submitted to the Office of Bilingual Education were unusually high, with 34.1 percent of the respondents indicating this to be the case. This item on the questionnaire had a nonresponse rate of 10.2 percent, which was the highest nonresponse rate on the entire questionnaire. The 10.2 percent of nonrespondents to the question of parent advisory councils existing prior to the preparation of the proposal submitted to the Office of Bilingual Education is alarming. If the nonrespondents did not know whether or not their respective councils existed prior to the preparation of the proposal, they were derelict in their responsibility to know the Bilingual Education Act and the rules developed by the U.S. Office of Education with respect to bilingual education and parent advisory councils. If, on the other hand, the nonrespondents did not wish to answer in the negative when, in fact, they were aware that their respective councils had not existed prior to the preparation of the proposal, these participants were concealing a violation by local school administrators and/or local school boards.

The 34.1 percent of respondents who indicated that their respective local education agencies were in noncompliance with the existence of parent advisory councils prior to the preparation of the proposal are to be commended for revealing conditions which definitely need investigation. Several questions come to mind when reviewing the fact that a little over one-third of bilingual projects do not have existing parent advisory councils prior to the preparation of the proposal. First, do these local education agencies in noncompliance ever convene an advisory group after the project is funded? Second, if, in fact, an advisory council is formed, it is just a rubber stamp for what has already been developed by the local school board and/or school administrators? Third, are the local education agencies in noncompliance only interested in federal funds without affording the parents of bilingual children an opportunity to participate in the development of the bilingual education program which will directly affect their children? Fourth, why has there not been closer scrutiny by the Office of Bilingual Education with respect to parent advisory councils? Fifth, why has there not been a booklet developed with general and specific guidelines (roles and functions) for parent advisory councils funded under Title VII? These questions are indeed very difficult to answer without doing objective research. Hopefully, if research is done to answer these questions, solutions will be developed to remedy the problems caused by the present lack of answers.

During the preparation of this paper, information was obtained from the Office of Bilingual Education which indicates an effort to ensure compliance by local education agencies with respect to parent advisory councils. Interim regulations for fiscal year 1978-79 have been developed in accordance with the Bilingual Education Act of 1978 and published in the *Federal Register* on March 29, 1979.

The interim regulations contain points which have been long overdue. Following are some of the highlights. Before the application is prepared, the applicant agency must form an advisory council with at least seven members. The majority of the advisory council must be composed of parents of children with limited English-speaking proficiency. Other members on the advisory council may be persons interested in bilingual education. The regulations now require that the advisory council participate in three ways: (1) assist in the planning of the project, (2) review drafts for the applicant agency, and (3) prepare comments on the application submitted to the Office of Bilingual Education.

The significant change in these interim regulations is that the applicant agencies must allow the advisory council to participate. The regulations also state that the applicant agency shall produce documentation that the advisory council did, in fact, participate in the development of the proposal. The applicant agency must also include comments on the application made by the advisory council with respect to the proposal. After the proposal has been reviewed by the Office of Bilingual Education and approved for funding, the regulations state that an advisory committee must continue in the participation of the bilingual program. Prior to these regulations, the language had not differentiated between an advisory council and an advisory committee. The difference now is that the advisory council participates in the development of the proposal and the advisory committee participates after the proposal has been accepted. A majority of the advisory committee must be parents of children with limited English-speaking proficiency. In bilingual projects that serve secondary school students, the regulations provide for secondary school students on the advisory committee. An advisory council member may also be a member of the advisory committee. Finally, assurances must be given by the applicant agency that after the application has been approved, the applicant agency shall provide for continuing consultation with and participation by the advisory committee.

These new regulations for applicant agencies with respect to parent advisory councils/committees indicate an effort by the Office of Bilingual Education to assure parent/community involvement in bilingual programs. The point must be made, however, that even though Congress has mandated parental involvement in bilingual programs and the Office of Bilingual Education has written regulations for applicant agencies ensuring parental involvement, there still exists a lack of specific roles and functions for parent advisory councils/committees.

In summary, as revealed by the study, councils not knowing their limits of authority have difficulty in fulfilling roles and in executing functions. Advisory councils, therefore, must know their specific roles and functions. Parent advisory councils/committees should not, however, operate unchecked. They should be evaluated on a continual basis with specified performance indicators. It is imperative to point out that before advisory councils/committees are evaluated, a complete program to familiarize the council/committee members with their responsibilities be initiated, that roles and functions be specified, and that goals and objectives be developed. Only then can objective evaluations of parent advisory councils/committees take place.

Editor's Note: On June 29, 1979, proposed rules for the Bilingual Education Program were published in the *Federal Register*. These rules, when finalized, will govern operation of the program beginning in fiscal year 1980. Regulations regarding parent advisory councils and committees remain basically the same as those presented in the interim regulations of March 29, 1979.

Notes

[1]*Elementary and Secondary Education Amendments of 1967, Statutes at Large* 81 (1968), 786.

[2]United States Office of Education, *Manual for Project Applicants and Grantees* (Washington, D.C.: Department of Health, Education, and Welfare, 1971), p. 67.

[3]United States, 93rd Congress, House of Representatives, 2nd Session, *Hearings before the General Subcommittee on Education of the Committee on Education and Labor* (Washington, D.C.: U.S. Government Printing Office, 1974), p. 108.

[4]United States, 93rd Congress, 2nd Session, *United States Code Congressional and Administrative News*, 1974 I (St. Paul, Minn.: West Publishing Company, 1975), p. 841.

[5]Gerald C. Sumner et al., *Federal Programs Supporting Educational Change, Vol. III: The Process of Change* (Santa Monica, Calif.: The Rand Corporation, 1975), p. III-4.

Parental Participation in Bilingual Education

Alberto M. Ochoa

Introduction

The primary tasks of schools are to develop the learning competence of students, to enhance the competence of students to cope with the demands of our society in which they must function, and to provide the satisfactions and a mentally healthy environment intrinsic to the well-being of all students (*White House Conference on Children and Youth*, 1970).

The enactment of federal and state educational legislation in the last ten years to assist schools in addressing the educational needs of underachieving and limited English-speaking students has sharpened awareness of the need to involve parents in the educational process of schools, in a collaborative relationship to provide the best possible education for these students.

This paper is intended for those who are interested in planning and implementing parent involvement at the district and local school levels. Experience has shown that while there is no lack of concern in the communities of limited English students and of students who are underachieving in school, those community members who assume collaborative responsibility with the school for improving its educational services are in need of skills to give their contribution a maximum usefulness. The same can be said of school personnel concerned with providing programs that have the input and support of the school community. It is hoped that this paper will help school personnel and bilingual program planners identify strategies and activities for involving parents in the educational process of schools.

The first part examines the need for parent participation in the education of their children and outlines a process for identifying the sociocultural characteristics of the school community—for curriculum planning, for understanding the cultural and social characteristics of the community, and for establishing a solid basis for the developing school-community relationship. The second part presents three approaches to involving the community in the development and implementation of educational programs that reflect the needs, wants, and concerns of parents. The third part suggests activities for generating parent involvement, interest, and support in the improvement of educational programs and curricula.

Parent Participation
in the Education of Children

There is a strong tradition in the United States that a public school should be responsible to the community it serves. Local school boards, PTAs, educational agencies, and the local school community all attest to the mainstream society's acceptance of this tradition. It fits well with society's view of itself as democratic; indeed, public education is counted among the most important of our democratic institutions (Rivera-Santos et al., 1978). "Democracy is government by the people in that it is the system within the people, the members of a community, who participate in the determination of policy for the community as a whole" (Cohen, 1961, pp. 316-317).

As Aleshire (1970) and Arnstein (1969) point out, in a democratic society the education of children requires that schools consider the following principles:

1. Educational planning should not be done without the participation of its clients.
2. Parental participation involves collective decision making, for the commitment made by the participants will motivate them toward practical implementation of planned action.
3. Parental participation ensures accurate decisions, speeds up the process of change, and creates active leadership. It provides a forum for the exchange of priorities.

Furthermore, Benellos (1971, p. 5) in addressing community involvement in a participatory democracy states that—

> Decision making is the process whereby people discuss, decide, plan, and implement those decisions that affect their lives. This requires that the decision-making process be continuous and significant, direct, rather than through representatives, and organized around issues instead of personalities.

It is not strange, therefore, that a growing body of judicial decisions and enacted legislation affirms the responsibility of public schools to all students. With respect to culturally and linguistically distinct students, Title VI of the Civil Rights Act of 1964; HEW May 25, 1970 Memorandum; *Lau* v. *Nichols* (1974); the Equal Educational Opportunity Act (1974); and the federally funded ESEA Title I and Title VII programs clearly require public schools to actively involve parents in the education of their children. Explicitly and implicitly, current law and state and federal mandates affirm that the instructional programs must take into consideration the concerns, the views, and the values of

the communities to which linguistically and culturally distinct
students belong. Widespread recognition exists that for a linguistically and culturally distinct student to experience school membership and
community identity as compatible and mutually supportive is certainly
a positive element in any school experience. In short, there are many
reasons why educational program planners, administrators, and
implementors need and seek an open, participatory, and collaborative
relationship with the communities of linguistically distinct students
(Rivera-Santos et al., 1978).

In regard to establishing school-community relationships, Clasky et
al. (1973, pp. 1-85) discuss four basic questions about school-community collaboration:

1. *Why collaborate?* To give people more voice in an institution
   that affects them. To reduce feelings of powerlessness and
   alienation resulting from unresponsive bureaucracies. To contribute to a "sense of community." To improve and coordinate
   the ways schools use community resources to enrich the school
   program.
2. *What conditions are necessary for effective collaboration?*
   People feel personal, group, and community interests are at
   stake so they identify a problem or goal and begin to prescribe a
   solution. They have a base of support, feel competent as a
   group, and operate well in an environment when there is a supportive climate and collaboration.
3. *What skills are necessary?* Communication skills and the ability
   to exchange ideas, information, criticisms person to person,
   person to group, and group to group. Planning skills. Leadership skills in defining problems, setting goals, examining alternatives, designing a strategy, assessing resource needs, designing evaluation.
4. *How do we judge success?* Successful collaboration can be
   measured in terms of purposes for school-community collaboration, e.g., through number/types of people involved in planning,
   evaluating, and implementing school programs; the number of
   opportunities for contributions; indicators of increased interaction and cooperative action; evidence of a comprehensive plan
   for public participation; and number/types of programs and
   personnel available to students.

Yet for many school administrators and teachers, the school-community collaboration is more easily sought than achieved. This is
evident in the frustration expressed by some professionals planning
bilingual education programs, and it is more sadly evident in existing
bilingual programs where the lack of real school-community participation and collaboration is apparent (Rivera-Santos et al., 1978).

Establishing School-Community Relationships

Gordon L. Lippitt (1965), in his discussion of school-community collaboration, feels that the desirable state of affairs is one in which there is trust established between the community and the school leadership. With reference to establishing an educational climate that is open, direct, trusting, and committed to the academic needs of linguistically and culturally distinct students, eight factors are suggested by Fox et al. (1975).

1. *Respect*   Schools should be places where there are self-respecting individuals, in a positive climate where there are no put-downs.
2. *Trust*   Trust is reflected in one's confidence that others can be counted on to behave in an honest way.
3. *High Morale*   People with high morale feel good about what is happening.
4. *Opportunities for Input*   Every person desires the opportunity to contribute his/her ideas and to know that they have been considered.
5. *Continuous Academic and Social Growth*   Each person needs to develop additional academic, social, and physical skills, knowledge, and attitudes.
6. *Cohesiveness*   Members should feel part of the school-community and should collaborate towards making the school run effectively.
7. *School Renewal*   Diversity and pluralism are valued. The school should be able to organize improvement projects rapidly and efficiently, with an absence of stress and conflict.
8. *Caring*   Every individual in the school should feel that other person(s) are concerned about him/her as a human being.

The eight factors are presented as applicable to the school organization and their quality as dependent on the practices and programs of the school operations. In reference to critical determinants that provide for a positive school climate, the following factors are discussed further by Fox et al. (1973, pp. 53-89):

1. Problem solving ability in which skills are adequately developed to reach effective solutions quickly. There should be well-developed structures and procedures for sensing the existence of problems, for inventing solutions, for implementing them, and for evaluating their effectiveness.
2. Improvement of school goals so that they are clearly stated and understood by all participants. Goals should serve as reference

points for making decisions, organizing school improvement projects, and guiding day-to-day operations.

3. Identifying and working with conflicts, recognizing that conflict is natural and that it occurs within individuals, between them, and between groups. Conflict is accurately identified and effectively worked on.

4. Effective communications which enhance interpersonal relationships, rather than causing alienation, isolation, misunderstanding, fear, and frustration. There should be emphasis on sharing and problem solving.

5. Involvement in decision making in which all participants have an opportunity to improve the school. Decisions should be based on pertinent information and decision processes that are clearly specified.

6. Autonomy and accountability which balance the freedom of being independent and self-governing with the necessity and desirability of being responsible for actions through reporting and explaining processes in achieving goals and objectives.

7. Effective teaching/learning strategies in which goals are clearly stated and educators seek evaluative feedback from students and community.

8. Ability to plan for the immediate and long-range future of the school.

According to Schmuck and Rundel (1972, pp. 2-13) schools, like other living systems, display different degrees of openness in communication and relationships within and between role groups. Increased contact and cooperation among the various role groups assist the entire school to learn to respond more adaptively to their needs. However, if school personnel are to be successful in establishing a positive school-community climate with linguistically and culturally distinct communities, they must be able to identify these communities.

An important step towards an understanding of the social, cultural, and political dynamics of the total school-community is to develop and implement a sociocultural survey. Such a survey can provide a realistic profile of the school community necessary for addressing the educational needs of linguistically and culturally distinct students.

Sociocultural Survey

Communities are dynamic, living organisms. No community, therefore, can be finally and completely known or described. Much can be learned, though, about a community's demographic and cultural characteristics, its patterns of influence, its associational patterns, and the psychological factors operating within it. Such knowledge about the community is vital for educators seeking to provide appropriate learning experiences for their students. There are several clear and sequential steps for developing a sociocultural description of a school community (Ochoa, 1975). The descriptive process is outlined as follows.

The sociocultural description should provide information needed to answer the following questions:

- What is community involvement?
- How does one establish relations with the community?
- How does one identify the needs and concerns of the community?
- How does one use community resources?

The person, persons, committee, etc., responsible for developing the sociocultural description should brainstorm possible answers to the following questions before beginning actual research for data. This step will help to organize the research that will follow. Questions to be brainstormed are:

1. *What Is Community Involvement?*
   A. What is the community?
   B. Who is the community for?
   C. How fast can a community change?
   D. What is the responsibility behind community involvement (rhetoric vs. action)?
   E. How can you facilitate the process of community involvement?

2. *How Do You Establish Relations with the Community?*
   A. Who are the key people in the community? the people of influence? the decision makers?
   B. What kind of influence do they assert?
   C. How do you become a member of the community? How can you become involved in the community? and with whom?
   D. What may inhibit you from establishing relations with the community?

3. *How Do You Identify the Needs and Concerns of the Community?*
   A. Where should you inquire about community needs? community concerns?
   B. What do you ask?
   C. Who are the spokespersons for the community?
   D. Who sets priorities in the community? How are priorities established?

    E. What are the needs and concerns of the community as you perceive them?

    F. What are the needs and concerns of the community as the community residents perceive them?

4. *How Do You Make Use of Community Resources?*
    A. What resources are there in the community that can be used to implement educational programs?
    B. What community resources help facilitate educational objectives?
    C. How do you use the community to enrich the school curriculum?
    D. What is the level of interest and commitment to the use of community resources? and by whom?

The research phase will develop information in five specific areas of the school community:

- Demographic characteristics
- Cultural characteristics
- Associational patterns
- Influence patterns
- Social-attitudinal factors

There are several questions for each of these areas (Ochoa, 1975). They can be answered from a number of sources which will be listed later. Because of the breadth of information required for the sociocultural description, it is recommended that different persons or groups be given responsibility for each of the five areas described above. The different persons or groups can then pool their information or prepare a descriptive community profile. The questions listed below should be taken as a guide; they should suggest others to the research participants.

1. *Demographic Characteristics*
    A. How many people live in the community?
    B. What proportion live together? What proportion live alone?
    C. What is the age distribution?
    D. What is the percentage of school-age children?
    E. What is the income distribution?
    F. What types of housing are available and where are they located?
    G. What proportion of the community receive welfare funds?
    H. How are the people employed? Do children work?
    I. How many people are unemployed?
    J. What levels of education are characteristic of various segments of the community?
    K. What religious groups are found in the community?
    L. What type of industry is present?

    M. What recreational facilities are available to the community? Where?

    N. What elementary and secondary schools are used by the community?

    O. What means of transportation are available?

    P. What hospitals, clinics, and other services are accessible to the community? What emergency services are available?

2. *Cultural Characteristics*

    A. What languages/dialects are spoken?

    B. How are families organized (e.g., what is the father role, mother role, child role)?

    C. Are families nuclear or extended?

    D. What ties are there to relatives?

    E. What recreation do families prefer?

    F. What material items do people value?

    G. What are the food preferences and eating habits?

    H. What holidays and events do the people consider important?

    I. What clothing and grooming are acceptable?

    J. What do family members discuss?

    K. What TV programs do they watch? Do they listen to radio/TV programs in languages other than English?

    L. What newspapers do they read? What magazines do they subscribe to?

    M. What do they normally eat for breakfast, lunch, and dinner?

    N. Are family activities centered around school, church, sports, or other members of the family?

    O. What are the religious practices of the community?

    P. Who are the apparent heroes—sport figures, politicians, movie stars, etc.?

    Q. What appear to be the spending patterns? Who is the breadwinner? What is the income level?

    R. What do the people perceive as their immediate problems?

    S. What types of music are popular?

    T. What is considered unfair and fair?

    U. What is considered insulting?

    V. What rituals mark birth, puberty, marriage, and death?

    W. What conduct merits scorn and ridicule?

    X. What modes of artistic expression are allowed or encouraged?

    Y. What is considered funny?

    Z. What folklore (stories, legends, music, dances, etc.) do community members know?

3. *Associational Patterns*

    A. Are there religious divisions? If so, what are they?

    B. Ethnic divisions?

    C. Neighborhood cliques?

    D. Who marries whom?

    E. What kinds of barriers to association exist?

    F. Are there important clubs and associations? Who is in and who is out of them?

    G. Who attends what religious services?

    H. Which groups buy at different shopping centers, the corner grocery store, etc.? Why?

    I. Who associates with whom in regard to social status, occupation, wealth, age, sex?

4.   *Influence Patterns*
   A.   What political systems exist?
   B.   Are there power blocks of labor? employers? businesspeople?
   C.   Do many people feel powerless? Why?
   D.   Are there noncitizens in the community?
   E.   Have any civil rights been violated? When and how?
   F.   Who are the influential people, groups, and associations in the community?
   G.   Who influences whom?
   H.   How does information flow through the community?
   I.   What groups are respected in the community? By whom?
   J.   What groups are *not* respected by the community? Why not?
   K.   Who are the decision makers—school board, local government, law enforcement, etc.? Are they representatives of the community?

5.   *Social-Attitudinal Factors*
   A.   What are the different stereotypes that the various categories of people have of others?
   B.   What self-concepts do the various categories of people have?
   C.   What is the social distance between the various categories of people?
   D.   Who feels "top dog"; who feels "underdog"? What evidence leads to this feeling?
   E.   What people or groups are considered agitators, radicals, troublemakers, etc.? Why?
   F.   What celebrations, demonstrations, incidents have taken place in the community that indicate what people in the community feel strongly about?
   G.   What is the awareness of social justice in the community (ways things should be)?
   H.   What are the community members' attitudes towards community change? Do they rely on tradition, fears, feelings that existing problems are unsolvable?
   I.   What are the community members' attitudes toward their living conditions? Are they perceived as problematic? Do they accept the state of conditions as they are? Are problematic conditions denied?

Some hard work and ingenuity will be required to develop the information required for the sociocultural description. Much information, however, can be gathered from sources such as:

- United States Census
- Community fact book (Chamber of Commerce)
- Annual city/county reports
- Historical documents of the area
- Local census information
- Information about community social services
- Demographic statistics
- Feasibility studies on housing, educational services, etc.
- Newspaper records
- Interviews with local officials, government personnel, librarians, educators, police officials, etc.
- City/county planning department

The results of such a sociocultural description can be of great value to planners of education programs for the culturally and linguistically distinct school/community and will provide the school with a solid basis for its developing school-community relationship. The descriptive profile, if made available to them, will also help community groups to assess their own needs and objectives—e.g., for child care centers, income tax services, voter registration, educational goals, etc. It will improve the school district's ability to tap community resources, enrich the curriculum, and assess educational goals and needs.

Involvement of Parents in the
Decision-Making Process

This section presents three approaches to involve parents in the decision-making process of the school or school district. The three approaches are:

1. Organizational approach for developing and implementing bilingual desegregation programs for national-origin minority communities (Institute for Cultural Pluralism/Lau Center Approach)

2. Community input process for curriculum development (Deni Leonard Model)

3. Community-school advisory council approach (San Diego Center for Community Education)

All three approaches have been implemented in a number of school communities and provide for the involvement of parents in determining the educational needs, wants, problems, and priorities for their children and in finding the ways to address their concerns. The first approach involves the culturally and linguistically distinct communities of the nation in the development and implementation of bilingual desegregation programs. The second approach addresses the involvement of the minority community in development of curriculum. The third approach provides a structure in the form of a school advisory council for advising the personnel of the school about the implementation of its instructional programs.

Organizational Approach for Developing and Implementing
Bilingual Desegregation Programs for National Origin Minority
Communities

For over three years the Institute for Cultural Pluralism through its National Origin Desegregation Center has implemented a comprehensive six-phase technical assistance process, in assisting school districts to comply with the *Lau* v. *Nichols* Supreme Court decision of 1974, that addresses the educational needs of students whose home language is other than English. This six-phase process (see Figure 1) outlines the development and implementation of a district-wide master plan for

FIGURE 1

**Six-Phase Technical Assistance Process for
Developing and Implementing a
District-Wide Educational Master Plan**

Notification of Noncompliance from Office of Civil Rights

PHASE I
Orientation to General Assistance Center and Title VI Remedies
GAC-District Letter of Agreement
Community Leaders Workshop

PHASE II
Establishment of Steering Committee

PHASE III
Needs Assessment

PHASE IV
Development of Master Educational Plan

PHASE V
Development of Timeline/ Management Plan

PHASE VI
Implementation of Educational Master Plan

meeting the linguistic and academic needs of Lau students.* During this process the input and participation of a community throughout the six phases is an ongoing task. The rationale for the participation of parents in the six-phase process is based on the following assumptions:

- Parents, by participating in the planning of an educational program, are more likely to promote the plan in the community at large and are more likely to work for a smooth and orderly implementation of the program.
- Parents who have participated in designing an educational program will be required to bear part of the responsibility for the success or failure of the program.
- Parents are in a unique position to offer the teacher valuable information about the learning styles and special needs of their children. In addition, it is through contact with parents and other community persons that teachers and administrators can come to understand the special features of a culture or lifestyle which may be different from their own.
- Finally, parents are a valuable resource in the classroom who can assist school personnel in providing the best possible education for all the children in the school.

Community Participation and Steering Committee   Community participation in the Lau Educational Master Plan development process begins with a district invitation to community leaders to participate in an orientation workshop. The six-phase educational planning process is discussed and the role of the steering committee is defined. The composition of the steering committee is decided; this normally reflects one of the three selection models shown in Figures 2, 3, and 4. The models differ in *school district* representation; in each case, *community* representatives are "selected by the community using its own method of selection." This initial workshop is an important one for community and district personnel alike; it must create a foundation for a working district-community partnership with all firmly committed to the development and implementation of an educational plan that genuinely reflects the needs, concerns, and strengths of school district personnel, community people, and students. Partnership is stressed; a steering committee established only to "advise and submit" will not generate from its members the energy and commitment necessary for its tasks. The steering committee must take part in all phases of the initial planning, implementing, monitoring, evaluation, and modification of the bilingual desegregation master plan.

The steering committee, once constituted, must receive inservice

---

*A Lau student is one whose home language is other than English, regardless of the language spoken by the student, and who is not performing conceptually and linguistically at a level equal to or better than the district standard of proficiency.

training to assure that all its members understand fully their functions, responsibilities, and activities.

Management of Bilingual Desegregation Educational Master Plan: Community Task Force Groups   As a means of functionally operating a bilingual desegregation steering committee, it is recommended that a "meet and confer" process of negotiating areas of disagreement be used (see Figure 5). "Meet and confer" means that the steering committee is encouraged to reach a consensus in making decisions rather than vote.

A recommended process for managing the bilingual desegregation steering committee in the development and implementation of a comprehensive educational plan is to divide the committee into task force groups (Figure 6). The task force groups are responsible for specific areas of the educational plan. The general areas that are included in any educational plan are—

- Language determination and language assessment
- Staff development and recruitment
- Administrative reorganization and allocation of resources
- Curriculum selection and program development
- Community relations
- Counseling and guidance
- Process and product evaluation

Members for each of the task force groups should be selected from the steering committee participants. Each group should include members from the target community *not* employed by the school district. (See Appendix A, page 76 for suggested activities of each task force group.)

Task Force Areas   The steering committee should be divided into the following areas, which constitute the key components of an educational plan:

1. *Language Determination*
   To improve techniques of student language identification, language proficiency, and oral language assessment procedures used by the school district.

2. *Staff Development*
   To identify staff development needs and recommend inservice training activities to meet the conceptual and linguistic needs of the identified students.

FIGURE 2

Model I for Selection of Title VI Lau
Steering Committee

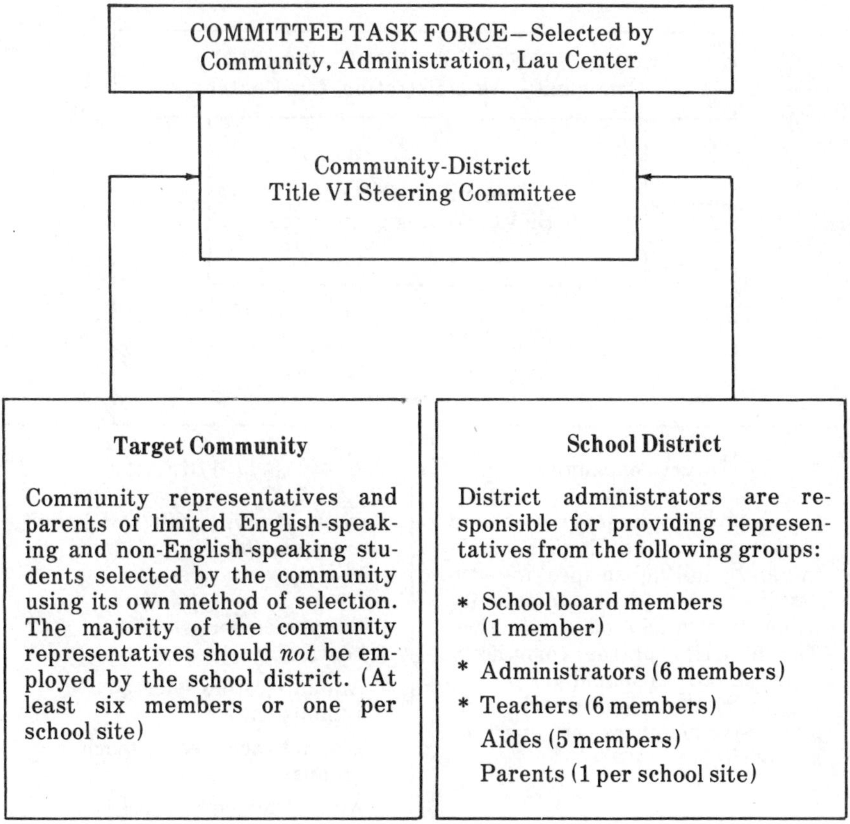

COMMITTEE TASK FORCE—Selected by
Community, Administration, Lau Center

Community-District
Title VI Steering Committee

Target Community

Community representatives and parents of limited English-speaking and non-English-speaking students selected by the community using its own method of selection. The majority of the community representatives should *not* be employed by the school district. (At least six members or one per school site)

School District

District administrators are responsible for providing representatives from the following groups:

* School board members
  (1 member)
* Administrators (6 members)
* Teachers (6 members)
  Aides (5 members)
  Parents (1 per school site)

*May designate an alternate

FIGURE 3

Model II for Selection of Title VI Lau
Steering Committee

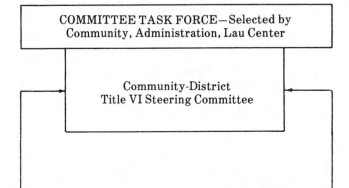

COMMITTEE TASK FORCE—Selected by
Community, Administration, Lau Center

Community-District
Title VI Steering Committee

Target Community	School District
Community representatives and parents of limited English-speaking and non-English-speaking students selected by the community using its own method of selection. The majority of the community representatives should *not* be employed by the school district. (At least six members or one per school site)	Various groups within the district are responsible for providing district representatives: * Board member selected by board of trustees * Administrators selected by administrators * Teachers selected by teacher groups Aides selected by classified employee groups Students selected by student body Parents selected by school or district advisory committees

*May designate an alternate

FIGURE 4

Model III for Selection of Title VI Lau Steering Committee

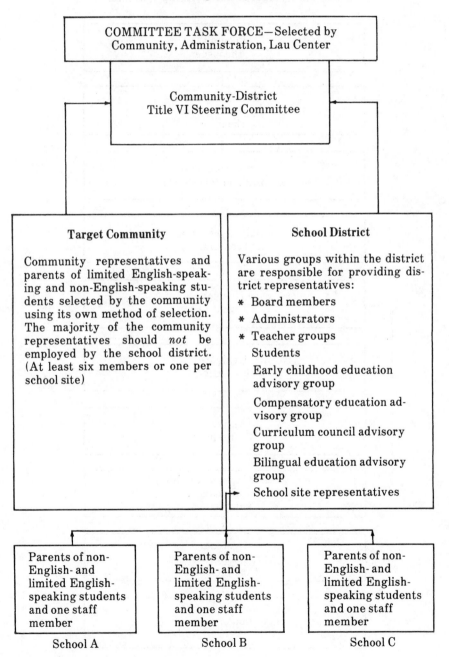

COMMITTEE TASK FORCE—Selected by Community, Administration, Lau Center

Community-District Title VI Steering Committee

Target Community

Community representatives and parents of limited English-speaking and non-English-speaking students selected by the community using its own method of selection. The majority of the community representatives should *not* be employed by the school district. (At least six members or one per school site)

School District

Various groups within the district are responsible for providing district representatives:

* Board members
* Administrators
* Teacher groups
  Students
  Early childhood education advisory group
  Compensatory education advisory group
  Curriculum council advisory group
  Bilingual education advisory group
  School site representatives

Parents of non-English- and limited English-speaking students and one staff member

School A

Parents of non-English- and limited English-speaking students and one staff member

School B

Parents of non-English- and limited English-speaking students and one staff member

School C

*May designate an alternate

FIGURE 5

**Recommended Decision-Making Process for the
Bilingual Desegregation Steering Committee**

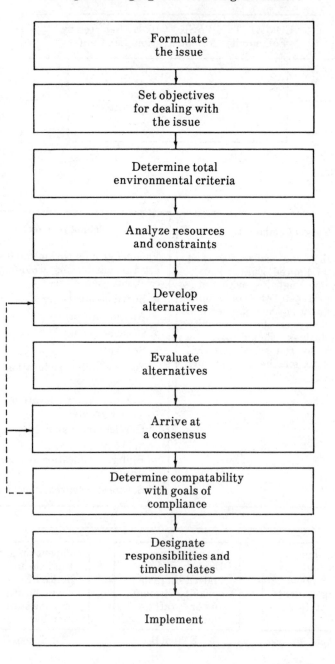

FIGURE 6

Establishment of Task Force Groups

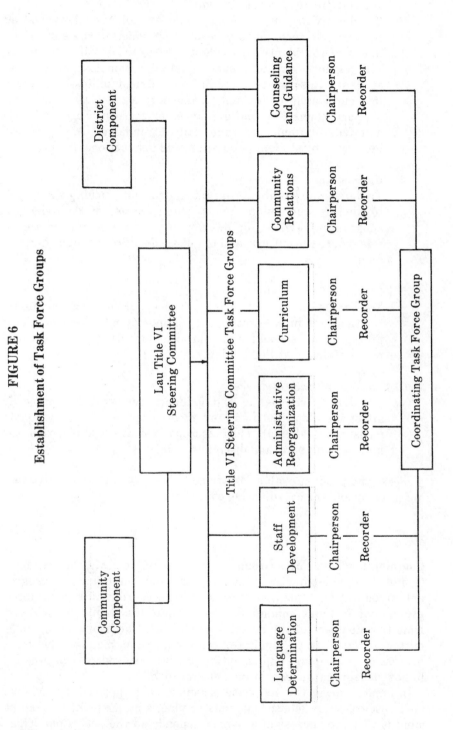

3. *Administrative Reorganization*

   To identify organizational procedures, policies, plans, and administrative techniques necessary for meeting the educational needs of the identified students. Also, to identify district resources necessary to ensure equal educational benefits for all students. Resources should include curriculum, inservice training, curriculum development, teacher salaries, administrative support, counseling and guidance services, utilization of state and federal funds, average daily attendance (ADA) monies generated by student population, and instructional facilities.

4. *Curriculum*

   To determine suitable program models and teaching strategies, to identify curriculum needs, and to assist in the selection, adaptation, revision, or development of curriculum materials relevant to the cultural and linguistic needs of the identified students.

5. *Community Relations*

   To provide the district with assistance in improving community relations and in integrating the community into the educational process of the school for the purpose of meeting the educational needs of the identified students.

6. *Counseling and Guidance*

   To identify counseling and guidance services that critically affect the identified Lau student in order to provide adequate measures to alleviate such discrepancies as racial isolation, the high dropout rate, and discipline problems.

Process and product evaluation are addressed by each respective task force group and the coordinating committee.

Coordinating Task Force Group   In order to facilitate the coordination of the development and implementation of the bilingual desegregation educational plan, a representative coordinating task force group that includes community representatives should be selected from the members of the steering committee. The coordinating committee function is to facilitate, coordinate, and manage the total process of developing, implementing, evaluating, and revising the bilingual desegregation educational master plan.

   In implementing the six-phase organizational approach for a bilingual desegregation educational master plan, a major point to keep in mind is that the success of any plan depends on the active participation and direct input of community leaders and parents who represent the various schools/communities of the district throughout the process.

Community Input Process for Curriculum Development

For too many years the local community has been ignored by professional educators who develop curriculum that does not include the language and culture of the minority communities (Leonard, 1974). In response to this failure, Deni Leonard developed a process to enable members of a local community to be involved in the development of school curriculum that considers the values of that community. The Community Input Process for Curriculum Development (Leonard, 1975) calls for the community to participate in the development of curriculum that reflects the values, lifestyle, language, and thought of the people in a community in cooperation with school district technicians. Leonard stressed the importance of a curriculum representative of peoples' lifestyles:

> Community spirit, or community thoughts, should become part of the curriculum. The children of the particular community will be better able to be given equal opportunity to participate in the educational process because they will not have to give up their nationality to be educated. (Leonard, 1975, p.3)

The Community Input Process for Curriculum Development is a twelve-part process which was developed at the University of Oregon in 1974. A major objective of this process is to teach the community the twelve-step curriculum development method in order for the curriculum developer to be used as a technician. Leonard further explains—

> Historically, the curriculum concepts were known only to the curriculum developer. Each curriculum concept was to be shared among curriculum developers only. Thus, many community members were unable to ask appropriate questions of the curriculum developer because they knew not what to ask. (Leonard, 1975, p.4)

Another important objective of the twelve-step method for curriculum development is to transfer curriculum skills to the community. The community is the decision maker about what concepts should be taught, how the curriculum is to be developed, and in general how a public school curriculum continuum should look.

Twelve-Step Method   The twelve-step method for curriculum development described by Deni Leonard (1975, pp. 6-8) involves the community in the development of curriculum products for use in the community school. The process outlines the steps for developing curriculum with control and support of the community. As part of the twelve-step method, a decision-making process (see Figure 7) is used. The consensus decision-making process enables participants to contribute to most of the decision-making of curriculum development.

The school-community process as described by Deni Leonard may seem alien and even threatening to some. However, the success in establishing a school-community relationship and in producing tangible resources for improving the quality of education makes a powerful argument that educational professionals should consider seriously. For as Leonard (1974) describes, in the implementation of the process, the American Indian community gained the knowledge and confidence to discuss education policy with top policymakers. Education technicians, in turn, learned that the community concerns in education were not unrealistic and that technicians were not members of the community until they joined the community, the community which welcomed them and learned from them.

Community School Advisory Council Approach

The community advisory council is a representative group of school community members committed to the common goal of community development through the identification of problems and the identification and implementation of solutions. As required by both federally and state funded educational programs, the function of advisory councils is to assist the school to improve instruction, auxiliary services, school environment, and school organization to meet the educational needs of students. In addition, most educational advisory councils are required to involve parents broadly reflective of the sociocultural and economic composition of the school attendance area. However, effectively using an advisory council involves hard work. Some process principles suggested by the San Diego Center for Community Education (Robbins et al., 1975, pp. vii-viii) are as follows:

1. People are more likely to accept a changed pattern of behavior when they, themselves, have participated in the planning.
2. People are more likely to change their behavior if they see that other people, like themselves, are also planning and endorsing such a change of behavior.
3. People are more likely to act upon a request if they can be per-

FIGURE 7

Decision-Making Process

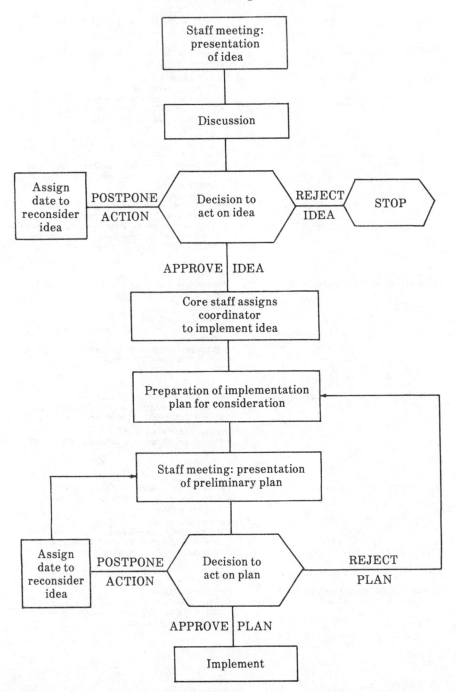

The Twelve-Step Method
Deni Leonard's Curriculum Development Model

Process	Description
1. Community meetings are held.	Meetings are held to determine the community's input to curriculum content. *Results and decisions:* • Curriculum is defined. • Priorities in curriculum content are defined. • A curriculum committee representing specific areas of the community is selected.
2. Community curriculum committee meetings are held.	*Results and decisions:* • Workshops are planned, conducted, and evaluated to teach members about curriculum development. • Area meetings are scheduled. • Recruitment methods are organized to ensure representation from the entire community. • An educational advisory board composed of federal, state, and local education officials and other professional educators is selected.
3. Area community meetings are held.	A meeting is held in each area of the community to specifically define curriculum content. *Results and decisions:* • Curriculum is defined. • A community educational needs assessment is completed. • Participants are asked to respond to the priorities established at the first community meeting.
4. Production of curriculum materials begins.	The technical development staff begins developing educational materials based on the priorities determined at the community meetings. *Results and decisions:* • Curriculum products are developed in prototype form.
5. Prototypes are bench tested.	The technical development staff hires an educational curriculum evaluation consultant to review the prototype products. *Results and decisions:* • If the products pass this evaluation, preparations for pilot testing are made; if not, products are revised and resubmitted for a bench test.
6. Prototype products are submitted to the curriculum committee.	*Results and decisions:* • If the products are approved, preparations for pilot testing are made; if not, products are revised and resubmitted for approval.

7. Curriculum products are pilot tested.

The products are tested with a limited number of potential users. The function of the pilot test is to provide information to the developers on how well the materials and procedures meet the objectives for which they were designed. Prototypes include teacher training manuals to introduce the teacher to instruction of the new products.

Results and decisions:
- Revisions are made based on the pilot test.

8. Curriculum committee consults with technical developers during the pilot test.

The curriculum products may go through several revisions reflecting the conclusions of the pilot test. The pilot test includes primary input from the curriculum committee.

Results and decisions:
- The committee makes decisions about the content of the curriculum during the pilot test to ensure community input.

9. After successful pilot testing, the curriculum products are presented to the curriculum committee and the educational advisory board.

Results and decisions:
- The advisory board provides information to their educational communities about availability of the materials, encouraging product acceptance and purchase.
- The two groups approve the materials as effective and ready for field testing, or they disapprove and request further revision and resubmittal.

10. Curriculum product is field tested.

Products are tested for effectiveness in actual classroom settings. Analysis and reporting of information provides the developers with feedback needed for final minor modifications. After completing field test, products are ready for widespread dissemination.

Results and decisions:
- Major teacher training takes place at the beginning of field testing.
- Final revisions are made.

11. Products are presented to the curriculum committee and the educational advisory board.

The two groups review field test results.

Results and decisions:
- The products are approved, or disapproved and a request is made for revision and resubmittal. Upon approval, the materials are ready for general use in the schools.

12. Products are presented to the curriculum committee for the last time.

Summative evaluation results are presented to the committee.

Results and decisions:
- The committee gives final approval of products.
- Products are ready for dissemination.

suaded to commit themselves to a positive decision at the time they hear the request.

4. The group itself can be used to stimulate consideration of the new action, to analyze the difficulties and suggest ways to overcome them, and finally to arrive at some decision about the action being discussed.

5. If free discussion of a proposed action results in some general agreement among group members that they will participate in this action, there is a good chance that the action will be carried out.

Above all, the main objective of a school advisory council, is to serve as the eyes and ears of the school principal. Some general activities of any advisory council are—

1. Keeping the principal informed of the school-community educational needs

2. Assisting in the planning and implementation of educational programs

3. Assisting in the identification of resources

4. Assisting in the evaluation of the school programs

5. Assisting in maintaining open and ongoing communication with the school/community

Establishment and Function of a School Advisory Council   Schools should be cautioned against establishing councils for self-serving reasons. Robbins et al. (1975, pp. 1-2) discuss five poor reasons for establishing community advisory councils which school administrators should avoid—

1. Free Labor: "If we had a community advisory council, maybe it could dig up the facts we need."

2. Rubber Stamp: "I'll bet my bottom dollar we could set up an advisory council to OK our new policies on discipline and get the parents to accept them, too."

3. Shock Absorber: "We've taken enough abuse on that issue. Let the community advisory council get some of the flak."

4. Front-man Promoter: "We've got to cut down again on those multicultural courses. Don't you think our advisory council could push them through next year?"

5. SOS Team: "We aren't getting anywhere with the fiscal people, and now we're in a head-on fight with the teachers. Don't you think a community advisory council could. . .?"

The purpose of an advisory council is to provide the school with input, ideas, and advice for improving the educational program and curricula of the school and not to function as operators or, in some cases, as backers of the status quo.

The composition of an advisory council generally has the following representation:

- Parents of pupils attending the school selected by such parents
- Community representatives not employed by the school
- Principal of the school
- Teachers selected by teachers at the school
- Students selected by students at the school (secondary schools)
- Other: service educational agencies and groups

The operation and success of any advisory council depends on the formulation and implementation of its bylaws. Burden and Whitt (1973), Robbins et al. (1975), and Whitt (1971) make the recommendations that in developing bylaws the advisory council should give particular attention to the following areas:

- Purpose: What are the goals and objectives of the council?
- Officers: Who will serve on the council (duties and responsibilities, term of office, and method of membership)?
- Membership: What will be the composition of and criteria for membership?
- Attendance: What process will be used to assure regular attendance on the part of all members?
- Meeting Requirements: When will the council meet?
- Task Force Subcommittee: What will be the areas of council activity?
- Amendment Process: What will be the mechanism to change or delete those sections of the bylaws not deemed necessary?
- Quorum: What will constitute a quorum to have an official meeting?

A sample of bylaws providing specific suggestions about the above questions appears as Appendix B.

Suggested Tasks for an Advisory Council   Each school/community has its own needs, wants, and problems in improving the educational programs, curricula, and services of its school. Thus, conducting a needs assessment within the school/community is a major function that is necessary to give the advisory council direction in its endeavors to improve or maintain the services of the school. Robbins et al. (1975, pp. 57-58) suggest the following tasks for a school advisory council to undertake:

1. Conduct, with resident assistance, a community needs assessment
2. Develop a list of priorities based upon needs, wants, and problems
3. Make recommendations about program development
4. Assist in establishing program goals and objectives
5. Determine a scheme for evaluating progress
6. Develop a system for community-school communication to promote publicity of existing programs
7. Promote activities for children and adults—the total community
8. Assist in fact finding
9. Coordinate community services and activities
10. Develop support for the community school program
11. Act as an information clearinghouse
12. Develop a community resource index and program
13. Encourage and provide special programs
14. Act as a sounding board for suggestions, ideas, and new programs
15. Address problems as natural and expected
16. Establish reference file on needs, wants, and problems of community individuals

The school advisory council is unique in each community, and, therefore, implementation will vary among communities. However, all schools/communities are capable of positive change in resolving their own concerns; all have social problems that are natural and expected. Thus, the school advisory council can serve as a vehicle for community people to determine their educational wants and needs and to establish ways in which the community can become the best it is capable of being.

Suggested Activities for Generating
Parent Involvement, Interest, and Support

Parent participation in the activities of the school is determined by the following factors (Anderson and Safar, 1967):

1. The extent of participation allowed by the school decision-making unit
2. The leadership of the school/community
3. The skills and knowledge of the parents about the school curricula
4. The degree and quality of parent participation
5. The influence of the parent group on the administration of the school

To maintain parental support, it is important to achieve a level of participation which parents feel contributes to (and which actually does contribute to) the improvement of programs and curricula.

Too often, school personnel are not able to involve parents in their school curriculum because they conclude that parents are minimally educated or not interested in the development of their children (Nelson and Bloom, 1973). Whether acknowledged or not, parents are part of the school program.

Generating Parent Interest and Involvement

Parents are an untapped resource and can be trained to work with children effectively in many areas of the curriculum. For example, skills that parents have developed in their careers provide the school with an open textbook in the world of work. Parents can assist students to explore career choices in the fields of farming, reporting, nursing, engineering, accounting, piloting, dentistry, etc. These skills have important implications for enabling students to become aware of career options in the world of work.

Beyond PTA meetings and parent-teacher conferences, Nelson and Bloom (1973) suggest the following types of parent involvement activities that a school can initiate:

- Conducting study groups to share child development ideas, children's concerns, and child rearing practices

- Establishing task groups to articulate school-community activities and resources
- Assessing the school's effectiveness in providing educational services to culturally and linguistically distinct students
- Sponsoring informal coffee klatches in the homes of parents to discuss parental concerns such as the academic achievement of their children, financial assistance to students wanting to pursue higher education, school-community issues
- Conducting minipresentations with students on their concerns to provide ways by which they can cope with these concerns
- Providing resources for demonstrating specific concepts in the classroom
- Serving as school-community aides as well as counselor aides
- Tutoring students in subject matter areas
- Developing curriculum materials that reflect and promote the school-community cultures
- Developing annual school site plans addressing the academic and linguistic needs of their children

For parents to be successfully involved in these suggested activities, school personnel must at all times provide courtesy, support, and respect to all community participants.

Also, in order to facilitate the participation of parents, services such as child care, transportation to and from the school, translation, information dissemination, and refreshments must be considered and provided as much as possible.

Generating Parent Support

As with any group of people, if parents are provided with information about the education of their children, they are more likely to participate in the school program. Thus, an imperative school activity is parent education in areas such as:

1. Understanding the sociocultural structure of the school/community
2. Developing strategies for establishing communication and trust
3. Establishing school-community roles in the education of their children
4. Developing decision-making skills such as consensus agreement and conflict resolution
5. Assessing resources, needs, and concerns

6. Developing an understanding of the change process in order to create change
7. Developing skills in conducting meetings, workshops, and study groups
8. Developing skills in the learning process and academic development of their children.

Through such parent education inservice activities, parents can feel more comfortable with the language process and structure utilized by the school system and enter into dialogue with its personnel.

Additionally, in generating active parental support, it is advisable for the school administrator to continually involve parents in resolving school-community problems and concerns. The following process provides for such an approach:

1. Identify a problem or area of weakness—one which you realistically think can be changed.
2. State a goal; describe what change you want to make.
3. Build a support group; include others who will work for and support your goal.
4. Identify people, resources, policies which may block you from achieving your goal and what you can do about them.
5. Identify people, resources, policies which will help you achieve your goal.
6. Identify the steps you will take to achieve your goal, stating who will do what and when it is to be done.
7. Identify how you will know when you have reached your goal.
8. Review and modify the steps in your plan as you work. Make changes in your plan if you need to.

The above process can be used to tackle such problems and concerns as improving school attendance, reducing vandalism, reducing racial conflict, coordinating community resources, improving school achievement and student attitude, reducing drug abuse, improving the lack of curriculum and materials for limited and non-English-speaking students, and other concerns affecting the school community. Also, in the initial use of the process, parents should begin with a tangible problem or concern rather than attempt to tackle a number of issues at once. Hopefully, the use of this type of process will involve many role groups in the school community, for the ownership of the problem or concern belongs to everyone in the school community. It is through a collaborative effort and active participation that the concerns of the school community are resolved and the improvement of educational services actualized.

APPENDIX A

Composition and Tasks of Task Force Groups

Language Determination Task Force

Composition:
  Parents
  Bilingual teachers
  Bilingual resource teachers
  School principal
  Paraprofessionals
  Students

Tasks:

1. Determine process for student identification.
2. Select and evaluate instruments, for student language assessment.
3. Define process for student language assessment.
4. Compile data on student language proficiency.
5. Determine personnel to conduct assessment.
6. Determine training needed to assure consistent results.
7. Oversee implementation process.
8. Provide for dissemination of information to parents concerning data collection, interpretation, and use of data.
9. Select and evaluate assessment instruments to determine conceptual skills of students.
10. Repeat steps 3-8 with reference to student conceptual assessment.

Staff Development Task Force

Composition:
  Parents
  School principal
  Elementary teachers
  Secondary teachers
  Paraprofessionals
  Students

Tasks:

1. Determine staff competencies necessary to meet student characteristics (language and instructional).
2. Identify profile of district personnel based on step 1.
3. Identify staff development needs.
   a. Identify existing district personnel resources.
   b. Identify district needs based on student characteristics and projected needs.
   c. Identify district personnel needs.
4. Define staff development alternatives to meet personnel needs.
   a. Management and differentiated staffings of school personnel
   b. Affirmative action
   c. Inservice training
   d. Ongoing development of competencies
   e. Process and content
      (1) Criteria for participation
      (2) Delivery of services
      (3) Outcome competencies
5. Determine resource personnel and programs needed by staff for meeting staff development and personnel needs.
6. Coordinate staff development activities within the district program.
7. Develop timeline to implement sequential career ladder, staff development activities.

Administrative Reorganization Task Force

Composition:
Parents
Director of educational services
Bilingual administrators
Coordinator of federal and state projects
School board member
Students

Tasks:

1. Determine administrative responsibilities, policies, processes that affect Lau students.

2. Determine district administrative structure/procedures for identifying and serving Lau students.
3. Determine district personnel necessary to serve Lau students.
4. Determine affirmative action necessary for staff recruitment and/or administrative reorganization.
5. Coordinate implementation and evaluation of all district programs and curricula designed to meet the needs of Lau students.
6. Organize information regarding Title VII steering committee activities and determine manner of presentation to board of education.
7. Develop process and procedure for evaluation design of services to Lau students.
8. Analyze fiscal resources to determine sources of funding for services to Lau students.
9. Plan data collection storage and dissemination system.

Curriculum Task Force

Composition:
Parents
Director of curriculum
School principal
Teachers
Paraprofessionals
Students

Tasks:

1. Determine curriculum needs based on student characteristics.
2. Determine curricula and materials that exist and are presently used in district programs.
3. Evaluate existing materials and instructional programs for biases/omissions.
4. Identify curriculum materials to be used; activities; experiences; concepts to be taught; sequence; learner objectives to reflect the academic and cultural (home culture) needs of Lau students.
5. Coordinate various program objective activities (such as ECE, Title I, ESAA, Title VII).
6. Develop program design, scope, and sequence.
7. Develop curricula to meet the ongoing needs of Lau students

through selection, adaptation, revision, or development of curriculum materials.

Community Relations Task Force

Composition:
    Parents
    Migrant teachers
    Community aides
    School principal
    District administrator
    Students

Tasks:

1. Plan and assist in gathering input for educational plan.
2. Survey parent attitudes and needs in regard to school programs and delivery of services for the Lau student.
3. Determine the various community groups within the broad community.
4. Identify key community agencies and/or organizations as curricula resources.
5. Determine amount and areas of parent involvement in school programs.
6. Establish procedures and methods for contacting and involving community groups (especially parents of Lau students) in the school curricula.
7. Determine process for reporting student and district cognitive and affective progress to individuals and/or community groups.
8. Plan and assist in conducting community meetings, in reporting progress of all district programs, and in implementing educational plan.

Counseling and Guidance Task Force

Composition:
    Parents
    Bilingual counselor
    School principal

Psychologist or counselor
Students
Paraprofessionals

Tasks:

1. Identify counseling and guidance needs based on student characteristics.
2. Define programs to meet specific Lau student needs.
3. Identify counseling and guidance services and processes provided to Lau students.
4. Identify and determine competencies required of counseling and guidance personnel (especially language and cultural sensitivity) to meet the needs of Lau students.
5. Identify and evaluate policies affecting Lau students in assignment to special programs, assignment of classes, discipline procedures, extracurricular activities.
6. Identify and evaluate placement and achievement instruments necessary to meet the needs of Lau students.
7. Identify resource personnel and procedures to enable the counseling and guidance staff to meet the educational needs of Lau students.

APPENDIX B

Sample Community Advisory Council Bylaws

Article I   **Name**
This organization shall be called the_____
Community Advisory Council.

Article II   **Purpose**
It shall be the purpose of this council:
1. To offer an opportunity for all people residing, work-
    ing, or having an interest in the community to co-
    operate in efforts to understand, analyze, and solve
    community problems.
2. To promote cooperation among organizations and in-
    dividuals interested in improving the quality of life in
    the community.
3. To secure democratic action in meeting local needs
    through existing agencies, organizations, and insti-
    tutions.
4. To collect and give to members and others complete
    and accurate information concerning community
    needs and the resources available for meeting these
    needs.
5. To identify potential community leaders and to de-
    velop their qualities of leadership for community
    betterment.

Article III   **Membership**
Section 1
Any person residing, working, or having an interest in
the _____ community may become an active
member.

Section 2
All groups active in the school will be represented on the
council. These include but will not be limited to:
a. Employment Task Force
b. Housing Task Force
c. Health Task Force
d. Youth Development Task Force
e. Teaching Staff
f. Preschool Services

    g. Elementary Student Body
    h. Senior Citizens
    i. Church Task Force

Article IV **Voting**
    Section 1
    Any parent or guardian having children in _____
    School, who are paid members, shall vote without restriction.

    Section 2
    The representative or his/her alternate of each group listed in Article III, Section 2, or any active group recognized by a majority vote by those attending a council meeting shall have one (1) vote.

    Section 3
    Any person not having children enrolled in _____
    School or not being an active member of one of the groups listed in Article III, Section 2, shall be able to vote after attending three (3) consecutive council meetings and paying a membership fee of 50¢ per person. Voting rights will be forfeited after missing three (3) consecutive council meetings.

Article V **Community Task Force**
    Section 1
    Each action committee shall engage in such activities as designated to that committee by the council.
    A. Health Task Force
      It shall be the duty of this task force to assess health conditions in the community, establish annual objectives, and carry on the necessary activities to achieve those objectives.
    B. Employment Task Force
      It shall be the duty of this task force to assess employment conditions in the community, establish annual objectives, and carry on the necessary activities to achieve those objectives.
    C. Education Task Force
      It shall be the duty of this task force to assess education conditions in the community, establish annual objectives, and carry on the necessary activities to achieve those objectives.

D. Housing Task Force
It shall be the duty of this task force to assess housing conditions in the community, establish annual objectives, and carry on the necessary activities to achieve those objectives.

Section 2

There should be at least six (6) members on each task force.

Section 3

Task forces shall meet as often as is deemed necessary by the task force members.

Section 4

Members of each task force shall select a chairperson and secretary from among the members of their task force. The chairperson of each task force shall become a member of the council.

Article VI **Election of Community Council Officers**
Section 1

The officers of the council shall include the President, Vice President, and Secretary-Treasurer.

Section 2

The candidates for officers of the organization shall be chosen by a nomination committee. This committee will be made up of three (3) people appointed by the council. There must be a minimum of two (2) candidates for each office. Candidates must be members of the council.

Section 3

The council shall fill all vacancies that occur during their tenure in office until the next election.

Section 4

The officers of the council shall hold office for two (2) years.

Section 5

The officers of the council will be elected in April of the election year.

Section 6

The council shall appoint, by February of the election year, candidates for each office.

Section 7

The general membership shall vote for officers by secret ballot during the third week of April. To insure a representative vote, the executive council will appoint an election committee which shall secure the vote of every fifth member according to alphabetical listing.

Section 8

Officers will be installed in May of the election year and take office in June.

Article VII   **Get-It-Done (G.I.D.) Task Forces**

Each G.I.D. Task Force will engage in activities which back up, support, help to implement, or evaluate the work of local community task forces.

Article VIII **Amendments**

These bylaws may be amended at any general meeting of the community council by a majority vote of those attending, provided that notice has been given the membership by the council, one month in advance of such meeting.

Article IX   **Provisions**

Section 1

The president of the council shall act as presiding officer at all general meetings.

Section 2

General meetings shall be called by the council.

1. Any task force may request the council to call a general meeting.
2. Any member of this council may submit a request to a task force to call a general meeting.
3. A majority vote of those members attending a general meeting shall be required for any action.

Section 3

The minutes of general meetings will be mailed to all members within twenty-five (25) days after each meeting.

Section 4

The council shall establish membership dues.

Section 5

All council monies shall be deposited in the _____ School Community Council Fund and all disbursements will require approval at a general meeting of the council.

Bibliography

Aleshire, Robert A. "Planning and Citizen Participation—Costs and Benefits and Approaches." *Urban Affairs Quarterly*, June 1970: p. 375.

Anderson, James G., and Safar, Dwight. "The Influence on Differential Community Perceptions on the Provision of Equal Educational Opportunities." *Sociology of Education* 40 (Summer 1967): pp. 219-30.

Arnstein, Sherry. "A Ladder of Citizen Participation." *JIAP*, 35 (July 1969): p. 217.

Benellos, George, and Roussopolus, Dimitrios. *The Case for Participatory Democracy*. New York: Viking Press, 1971.

Burden, Larry, and Whitt, Robert L. *The Community School Principal: New Horizons*. Midland, Michigan: Pendell Publishing Co., 1973.

Clasky, Miriam, et al. *Together: Schools and Communities*. Boston: Advisory Council of Education, 1973.

Cohen, Carl. *Democracy*. New York: Macmillan Co. 1961.

Fox, Robert S., et al., eds. *School Climate Improvement: A Challenge to the School Administration*. Denver: Charles F. Kettering Foundation, 1975.

Leonard, Deni. *An Intercultural Community-Input Process for Curriculum Development*. Seattle: Resource Development Co., 1975.

Lippitt, Gordon L. *Nations Cities Magazine* 3, no. 12 (December 1965).

Lurie, Ellen. *How to Change the Schools*. New York: Random House, 1970.

Nelson, Richard C., and Bloom, John W. "Issues and Dialogue: Guiding Parent Involvement." *Elementary School Guidance and Counseling* 8, no. 1 (October 1973): pp. 43-49.

Ochoa, Alberto. *A Socio-Cultural Description of the School/Community*. San Diego: Multicultural Department, San Diego State University, 1975.

Robbins, Wayne R., et al. *A Guide for Community School Advisory Councils*. San Diego: Center for Community Education, 1975.

Rivera-Santos, Iris; Williams, Byron; and Ochoa, Alberto. *Manual V: Planning and Implementation Issues in Bilingual Education Programming*. San Diego: Lau Center, Institute for Cultural Pluralism, San Diego State University, 1978.

Schmuck, Richard A., and Rundel, Phillip. *Handbook of Organizational Development in Schools*. Palo Alto: National Press Books, 1972.

Whitt, Robert L. *Handbook for the Community School Director*, Midland, Michigan: Pendell Publishing Company, 1971.

White House Conference on Children and Youth. Report of Forum 14. Washington, D.C.: United States Office of Education, 1970.

About the Authors

Dr. María Estela Brisk is the director of bilingual education at Boston University where she also serves as associate professor in the Department of Education. She received her undergraduate degree in English from the University of Cordoba, Argentina. Her master's degree in applied linguistics is from Georgetown University, and she holds a Ph.D. in education from the University of New Mexico.

María B. Cerda is former executive director of the Latino Institute, a technical assistance resource center that provides leadership training, organizational development, and research programs for the Latino community in Chicago. She is a member of the Presidential Commission for the International Year of the Child. In 1969 Ms. Cerda became the first Latino to serve on the Chicago Board of Education. A founding member of ASPIRA of Illinois, Inc., she holds a B.A. in psychology from the University of Puerto Rico and a master's in social service administration from the University of Chicago.

Dr. Norberto Cruz, Jr., is an administrator in the Fairfax County Public School System, Virginia. A former teacher of Spanish, French, and English as a second language, Dr. Cruz has a special interest in bilingual education and the rights of parents with children enrolled in bilingual programs. He initiated and completed the first nationwide study to identify specific roles and functions of parent advisory councils serving Spanish-English Title VII bilingual education programs. He holds B.S. and M.S. degrees from Northwest Missouri State University and an Ed.D. from Virginia Polytechnic Institute and State University.

Dr. Alberto M. Ochoa directs the National Origin Desegregation Center and is an assistant professor in the multicultural department at San Diego State University. He holds B.A. degrees in sociology and Latin American studies from California State University at Los Angeles. His master's degree in special education is from the University of Southern California, and his Ed.D., with an emphasis in international education, is from the University of Massachusetts.

Dr. Jean J. Schensul directs her own technical assistance and evaluation firm Research in Action, located in Hartford, Connecticut. She also serves on the Hispanic Health Council as a coordinator of research and program development. In 1976 she was program developer and research consultant at the Center for New Schools in Chicago. Dr. Schensul holds a master's and a Ph.D. in anthropology from the University of Minnesota; she received her B.S. in anthropology and English literature from the University of Manitoba, Canada.

Kennith H. York directed the Bilingual Education for Choctaws of Mississippi (BECOM) project from 1974-77. He is the current director of the Choctaw Vocational/Technical Education Project of the Mississippi Band of Choctaw Indians and a former director of the Bilingual Bicultural Teacher Training Project at Mississippi State University. Mr. York has an M.A. in educational administration from the University of Minnesota and is completing his doctoral studies at that institution.